Kahoot!
QUIZ TIME
SPACE

DK

Contents

Introduction

What's in the middle of the Milky Way? How many tails does a comet have? What does an astronaut's backpack contain? Test your space knowledge in this quiz book, packed with questions and facts.

Delve into the wonders of space exploration, with everything from black holes and rockets to the International Space Station.

Keep score

Most quizzes in this book have 10 questions each. To keep score, you'll need to record the number of correct answers each player gets after each quiz.

Keep track on a piece of paper or even on a spreadsheet. Be sure to tally up the score for each quiz in order to crown the ultimate winner based on who gets the highest score from all 30 quizzes. Who will grab the gold medal?

Find more quizzes!

Look for QR codes throughout the book. Scan them to find exclusive online quizzes on the same theme. You can also head over to www.kahoot.com to discover more than 100 million quizzes on loads of interesting subjects!

Find 15 QR codes like this one on the pages that follow.

Make your own

Once you've completed these quizzes, get inspired to create your own on kahoot.com!

First, plan out your questions on paper and check out our top tips to make your quiz the best it can be. When it's ready, share your quiz with friends and family.

Don't worry about who wins or if your quiz doesn't turn out exactly how you planned. The important thing is to have fun . . . but it's even more important to stay safe online. Never share any personal information with anyone online and always use the internet with a trusted adult.

Top tips

1 Do your research and always check your facts with three trusted online sources.

2 Give your quiz a fun theme and vary your questions so the quiz doesn't get repetitive.

3 Include three or four multiple choice options, plus a few true or false and picture rounds.

Solar System

You'll be pleased you made space in your day for this out-of-this-world quiz . . .

1 **What does the Solar System revolve around?**
- ◆ Earth
- ▲ The Sun
- ● The Moon

2 **True or false: There are seven planets in the Solar System.**
- ◆ True
- ▲ False

3 **What is the nearest neighbor to Earth?**
- ◆ The Sun
- ▲ Saturn
- ● Mars
- ■ The Moon

4 **Which planet is closer to the Sun?**
- ◆ Mars
- ▲ Neptune
- ● Saturn

5 **True or false: A galaxy is a collection of billions of stars.**
- ◆ True
- ▲ False

6 **What is an asteroid?**
- ◆ A giant rock
- ▲ A type of star
- ● A galaxy
- ■ A spacecraft

7 Put these planets in order from smallest to biggest:
◆ Earth
▲ Neptune
● Mercury
■ Jupiter

8 Put the four inner planets in their correct order from the Sun.
◆ Mars
▲ Earth
● Venus
■ Mercury

9 The four outer planets are called . . .
◆ Far away planets
▲ Giant planets
● Big burper

Did you know?
The Solar System is a vast disc of material more than 19 billion miles (30 billion km) across.

Scan the QR code for a Kahoot! about the Solar System.

10 The Solar System was formed from dust and gas. When did this happen?
◆ 600 years ago
▲ 20,000 years ago
● 4.6 billion years ago

Turn to page 8 for the answers!

Solar System Answers

1 **What does the Solar System revolve around?**

▲ The Sun

Everything in the Solar System is held in place by the Sun's gravity.

2 **True or false: There are seven planets in the Solar System.**

▲ False

There are eight planets and their moons. There are also dwarf planets and other small bodies.

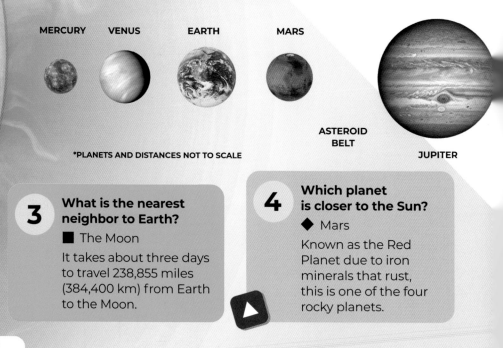

THE SUN

MERCURY   VENUS   EARTH   MARS

ASTEROID BELT

*PLANETS AND DISTANCES NOT TO SCALE

JUPITER

3 **What is the nearest neighbor to Earth?**

■ The Moon

It takes about three days to travel 238,855 miles (384,400 km) from Earth to the Moon.

4 **Which planet is closer to the Sun?**

◆ Mars

Known as the Red Planet due to iron minerals that rust, this is one of the four rocky planets.

5 True or false: A galaxy is a collection of billions of stars.

◆ True

Our Solar System is a small part of the Milky Way galaxy.

6 What is an asteroid?

◆ A giant rock

The Asteroid Belt is part of the Solar System between Mars and Jupiter.

7 Put these planets in order from smallest to biggest:

● Mercury
◆ Earth
▲ Neptune
■ Jupiter

Jupiter's diameter is about 11 times bigger than Earth's.

8 Put the four inner planets in their correct order from the Sun.

■ Mercury
● Venus
▲ Earth
◆ Mars

Mercury is the fastest planet, moving at 29 miles (47 km) per second.

9 The four outer planets are called . . .

▲ Giant planets

They are Jupiter, Saturn, Uranus, and Neptune. They all have rings.

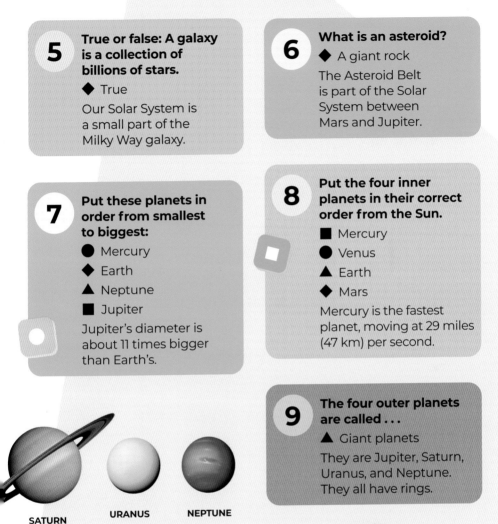

SATURN   URANUS   NEPTUNE

Podium!
Bronze: 1–5 correct answers
Silver: 6–8 correct answers
Gold: 9–10 correct answers

10 The Solar System was formed from dust and gas. When did this happen?

● 4.6 billion years ago

About 100 small planets collided to form the four rocky inner planets.

Moon

Test your Moon knowledge any time—night or day. You could be a howling success!

1 **True or false: The Moon is smaller than Earth.**
◆ True
▲ False

2 **The Moon's surface is pitted with . . .**
◆ Forests
▲ Craters
● Football pitches

4 **Put these layers of the Moon in order from inner to outer:**
◆ Mantle
▲ Crust
● Inner core
■ Lower mantle

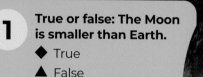

3 **When you look at the Moon, what are the dark areas you see called?**
◆ Swamps
▲ Seas
● Deserts

5 **True or false: The Moon's atmosphere is called an exosphere.**
◆ True
▲ False

Did you know?

Because of the Moon's weak gravity, an astronaut on the surface could jump six times higher on the Moon than on Earth.

6 How many Earth days is a day on the Moon?

◆ 5
▲ 18
● 20
■ 27

7 The Moon's gravity causes what on Earth?

◆ Tides
▲ Wind
● Rainfall
■ Temperatures

8 True or false: The Moon goes through a cycle of "phases," during which its shape appears to change.

◆ True
▲ False

9 What is it called when over half of the Moon's face can be seen?

◆ Waxing
▲ Waning
● Gibbous
■ Nearly full

10 True or false: This picture of the Moon shows a New Moon.

◆ True
▲ False

Turn to page 12 for the answers!

Moon Answers

1 **True or false: The Moon is smaller than Earth.**
◆ True
The Moon is a quarter as wide as Earth, but it is the largest and brightest object in the night sky.

2 **The Moon's surface is pitted with . . .**
▲ Craters
These have been made by meteorites when they hit the surface.

3 **When you look at the Moon, what are the dark areas you see called?**
▲ Seas
These are large areas of solidified lava that came from volcanoes billions of years ago.

4 **Put these layers of the Moon in order from inner to outer:**
● Inner core
■ Lower mantle
◆ Mantle
▲ Crust
The center of the Moon is a ball of incredibly hot, solid iron.

5 **True or false: The Moon's atmosphere is called an exosphere.**
◆ True
It is so thin that it gives no protection against heat from the Sun or colliding meteorites.

6 How many Earth days is a day on the Moon?

■ 27

A Moon day is the time the Moon takes to rotate once on its axis.

7 The Moon's gravity causes what on Earth?

◆ Tides

When the Moon, Sun, and Earth line up we have very high tides, known as spring tides.

8 True or false: The Moon goes through a cycle of "phases," during which its shape appears to change.

◆ True

During the cycle, we see different parts of the Moon lit by the Sun. Each shape is a phase.

9 What is it called when over half of the Moon's face can be seen?

● Gibbous

A Gibbous Moon is the phase both before and after a Full Moon.

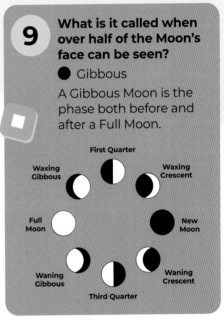

First Quarter

Waxing Gibbous

Waxing Crescent

Full Moon

New Moon

Waning Gibbous

Waning Crescent

Third Quarter

10 True or false: This picture of the Moon shows a New Moon.

▲ False

This is a Full Moon. A New Moon is when it first appears as a slender crescent.

Podium!

Bronze: 1–5 correct answers

Silver: 6–8 correct answers

Gold: 9–10 correct answers

Stars

Want to be a star? One in a million? Use all your flare to shine at this quiz.

1 **True or false: There are different types of stars.**
◆ True
▲ False

2 **Which of these is the name of a star?**
◆ Small purple
▲ White dwarf
● Tiny Tim
■ Yellow blob

3 **What is a constellation?**
◆ A group of planets
▲ Stars that form a shape
● A shower of meteorites

4 **A supernova happens when . . .**
◆ A star dies.
▲ Stars collide.
● A star is hit by a meteorite.

5 **Most stars are born in a huge cloud of gas and dust. What is it called?**
◆ A galaxy
▲ A solar system
● A satellite
■ A nebula

6 What color are the largest stars in the Universe?

◆ Pink
▲ Purple
● Green
■ Red

7 True or false: The smaller a star is, the longer it burns.

◆ True
▲ False

8 How would neutron stars be described?

◆ Small and heavy
▲ Big and lightweight
● Big and heavy

9 What are ball-shaped groups of stars called?

◆ Star balls
▲ Globular clusters
● Bunches

Did you know?

A star's color depends on how hot its surface is. The hottest stars produce a bluish light, while cooler stars are an orangish red.

Scan the QR code for a Kahoot! about stars.

Turn to page 16 for the answers!

10 Put these stars in order of size, from smallest to largest:

◆ Blue hypergiant
▲ Red supergiant
● Blue supergiant

Stars
Answers

1 **True or false: There are different types of stars.**
◆ True
Stars change the way they look and are given different names at various stages in their life cycle.

2 **Which of these is the name of a star?**
▲ White dwarf
This is the name given to a star in its final stage.

3 **What is a constellation?**
▲ Stars that form a shape
Constellations often have mythological names, such as Orion (pictured below) who was a hunter in Greek mythology.

4 **A supernova happens when . . .**
◆ A star dies.
A supernova is a mega explosion that happens when a star suddenly collapses. It can light up the Universe for days or even months.

5 Most stars are born in a huge cloud of gas and dust. What is it called?

■ A nebula

The nebula shrinks and forms clumps that become hotter and hotter until stars are formed.

6 What color are the largest stars in the Universe?

■ Red

The red supergiant nearest to Earth is Antares, and it is 57,000 times brighter than the Sun.

7 True or false: The smaller a star is, the longer it burns.

◆ True

Small stars are cooler, so they burn fuel more slowly than large stars.

8 How would neutron stars be described?

◆ Small and heavy

They are covered by an iron crust that is 10 billion times stronger than steel.

9 What are ball-shaped groups of stars called?

▲ Globular clusters

A single cluster can contain millions of stars that all formed at the same time.

Podium!

Bronze: 1–5 correct answers
Silver: 6–8 correct answers
Gold: 9–10 correct answers

10 Put these stars in order of size, from smallest to largest:

● Blue supergiant
◆ Blue hypergiant
▲ Red supergiant

Red stars are bigger than blue ones of the same brightness.

Comets and Meteors

Zap through this quiz like
a shooting star in the night sky,
leaving a trail of right answers!

1 **What are meteorites?**
◆ Dying stars
▲ Space rocks
● Bits of planet
■ Old spacecraft

2 **When a meteorite hits a planet what happens?**
◆ The planet wobbles.
▲ A crater is formed.
● It bounces back into space.

3 **Meteors are specks of dust that hurtle through the sky leaving a brief, bright trail. What else are they called?**
◆ Night lights
▲ Rubble rings
● Shooting stars

4 **What is named after the astronomer Edmond Halley?**
◆ A meteorite
▲ A planet
● A comet

5 **How many tails does a comet have?**
◆ One
▲ Two
● Three

6 True or false: Many comets come from a vast cloud.
◆ True
▲ False

7 When does a comet get its tails?
◆ It always has them
▲ When it's close to the Sun
● When it enters Earth's atmosphere

Did you know?
Thousands of meteorites land on Earth each year. Most land in seas or in deserts.

8 Comets leave a dust trail as they speed through the sky. What is this called?
◆ A rock storm
▲ A meteor shower
● Hail
■ Leftovers

9 Where was the first meteorite crater to be found on Earth?
◆ The US
▲ Thailand
● Australia
■ China

10 True or false: A meteor that reaches Earth's surface is then called a meteorite.
◆ True
▲ False

Turn to page 20 for the answers!

Comets and Meteors
Answers

1 What are meteorites?
▲ Space rocks
They are the debris that was left over when the planets formed.

2 When a meteorite hits a planet what happens?
▲ A crater is formed.
This is called an impact crater.

3 Meteors are specks of dust that hurtle through the sky leaving a brief, bright trail. What else are they called?
● Shooting stars
Their trails form as their outer layers burn away in Earth's atmosphere.

4 What is named after the astronomer Edmond Halley?
● A comet
Named Halley's comet, he calculated that it would be visible from Earth every 76 years.

5 How many tails does a comet have?
▲ Two
Most comets have one tail made of gas and one made of dust.

6 True or false: Many comets come from a vast cloud.

◆ True

The cloud is called Oort Cloud and exists far beyond the planets.

7 When does a comet get its tails?

▲ When it's close to the Sun

Comets develop tails as the ice in them warms up and releases gases and dust.

8 Comets leave a dust trail as they speed through the sky. What is this called?

▲ A meteor shower

These happen when Earth passes through the trail of dust left by a comet.

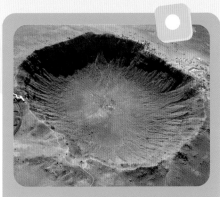

9 Where was the first meteorite crater to be found on Earth?

◆ The US

The Barringer Crater in Arizona is more than 0.7 miles (1 km) wide.

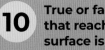

10 True or false: A meteor that reaches Earth's surface is then called a meteorite.

◆ True

About 110 tons (100 tonnes) of meteors collide with Earth each day. This is about the same weight as 20 elephants!

Podium!
Bronze: 1–5 correct answers
Silver: 6–8 correct answers
Gold: 9–10 correct answers

Astronaut Equipment

Are you dressed for space success?
Grab a pen, make some space,
and see if this quiz suits you.

1 **What do the letters stand for in EVA suit?**
◆ Eco Venus Astro
▲ Extra Venus Alarm
● Extra-Vehicular Activity

2 **Why do some astronaut spacesuits have stripes?**
◆ It's fashionable
▲ So they can tell each other apart
● To show what rank they are

3 **True or false: Inside an astronaut's helmet is a small foam block they can use to scratch an itchy nose!**
◆ True
▲ False

4 **Under their spacesuits, astronauts wear cooling garments filled with . . .**
◆ Feathers
▲ Tubes
● Pockets

5 **What do astronauts do with their dirty clothes?**
- ◆ Wash them
- ▲ Keep wearing them
- ● Throw them away

6 **What does an astronaut's backpack contain?**
- ◆ Life support system
- ▲ Communication system
- ● Tools
- ■ Sunglasses

7 **What is the Snoopy cap?**
- ◆ A dog hat
- ▲ A communication system
- ● A shower cap
- ■ A night cap

8 **The gold coating on the helmet's visor acts like . . .**
- ◆ Sunglasses
- ▲ A camera
- ● Contact lenses

Did you know?
A spacesuit weighs about 280 lb (127 kg) on Earth, but in space, it weighs nothing!

9 **True or false: Astronauts wear heated gloves.**
- ◆ True
- ▲ False

Scan the QR code for a Kahoot! about astronauts.

10 **In which order would you put these on?**
- ◆ Backpack
- ▲ Cooling garment
- ● Spacesuit

Turn to page 24 for the answers!

Astronaut Equipment
Answers

1 **What do the letters stand for in EVA suit?**
● Extra-Vehicular Activity

EVA suits are worn when astronauts are working outside their spacecraft.

2 **Why do some astronaut spacesuits have stripes?**
▲ So they can tell each other apart

This is especially helpful when more than two astronauts are working outside together.

3 **True or false: Inside an astronaut's helmet is a small foam block they can use to scratch an itchy nose!**
◆ True

Astronauts can't take off their helmets to scratch if they're working outside.

4 **Under their spacesuits, astronauts wear cooling garments filled with . . .**
▲ Tubes

These are sewn into the garments and filled with water to help keep the astronaut cool.

5 **What do astronauts do with their dirty clothes?**
● Throw them away

Astronauts cannot do laundry in space. They wear clothes until they become too dirty or smelly and then put them in the trash.

6 What does an astronaut's backpack contain?

◆ Life support system

It contains everything the astronaut needs to stay alive, including an oxygen supply.

7 What is the Snoopy cap?

▲ A communication system

It was a communication cap worn under a space helmet. New style suits have an audio system inside the helmet.

8 The gold coating on the helmet's visor acts like . . .

◆ Sunglasses

The movable visor and sunshade protect the astronaut from the Sun's rays.

9 True or false: Astronauts wear heated gloves.

◆ True

It gets really cold in space, so astronaut gloves have heated rubber fingertips.

Podium!

Bronze: 1–5 correct answers
Silver: 6–8 correct answers
Gold: 9–10 correct answers

10 In which order would you put these on?

▲ Cooling garment
● Spacesuit
◆ Backpack

Putting on all the layers of a spacesuit takes around 45 minutes.

Technology

Don't worry—you don't need to be a rocket scientist to do this quiz!

1 **What do scientists use to study space from Earth?**
- ◆ Telephones
- ▲ Telescopes
- ● Television

2 **Telescopes collect light to create an image. What do they use to do this?**
- ◆ Light bulbs
- ▲ Silver foil
- ● Mirrors

3 **What was the name of the first laptop that went into space?**
- ◆ Pear-I
- ▲ Hi-tech
- ● Shuttle Boom
- ■ GRiD Compass

4 **How long is the Hubble Telescope?**
- ◆ 16 ft (5 m)
- ▲ 43.3 ft (13.2 m)
- ● 72 ft (22 m)

5 **What is the Gaia spacecraft doing?**
- ◆ Contacting aliens
- ▲ Mapping the Milky Way
- ● Taking people to Mars

6 True or false: Gaia looks at 1 million stars every day.

◆ True

▲ False

Did you know?
The world's largest telescope, which is being built in Chile, is the Extremely Large Telescope (ELT). It will be as tall as a 15-story building, and its enormous mirror will gather more light than all 13 of the world's current largest telescopes put together.

8 What do the initials MRO stand for in space technology?

◆ Major Relay Orbiter

▲ Mars Reconnaissance Orbiter

● Manual Returning Orbiter

■ Mass Radio Orbiter

7 What is the James Webb Space Telescope?

◆ A powerful space telescope

▲ One of the first telescopes

● A handheld telescope for astronauts

9 True or false: Astrodog robots live on the International Space Station (ISS).

◆ True

▲ False

10 Which telescope has been repaired in space?

◆ None

▲ Hubble

● James Webb

Turn to page 28 for the answers!

Technology
Answers

1 **What do scientists use to study space from Earth?**

▲ Telescopes

Infrared and radio telescopes are two types of telescopes scientists use.

2 **Telescopes collect light to create an image. What do they use to do this?**

● Mirrors

Some telescopes use dozens of small mirror segments to make one large mirror.

4 **How long is the Hubble Telescope?**

▲ 43.3 ft (13.2 m)

It is about the length of a tourist bus.

3 **What was the name of the first laptop that went into space?**

■ GRiD Compass

It went into space on a space shuttle in 1983.

5 What is the Gaia spacecraft doing?

▲ Mapping the Milky Way

Gaia began its observations in 2014.

6 True or false: Gaia looks at 1 million stars every day.

▲ False

It can observe about 40 million stars a day.

8 What do the initials MRO stand for in space technology?

▲ Mars Reconnaissance Orbiter

This spacecraft, which launched in 2005, studies the geology and climate of the planet Mars.

7 What is the James Webb Space Telescope?

◆ A powerful space telescope

It was launched in 2021 and NASA released the first images from it in 2022.

9 True or false: Astrodog robots live on the International Space Station (ISS).

▲ False

Astrodogs don't exist, but Astrobees have flown around the ISS since 2019.

10 Which telescope has been repaired in space?

▲ Hubble

It has been repaired five times by astronauts.

Podium!
Bronze: 1–5 correct answers
Silver: 6–8 correct answers
Gold: 9–10 correct answers

Milky Way

The Milky Way is amazing! How much do you know about the galaxy you live in?

1 Put these in order from biggest to smallest:
- ◆ Galaxy
- ▲ Universe
- ● Solar System

2 True or false: At night you can see the Milky Way?
- ◆ True
- ▲ False

3 What is in the middle of the Milky Way?
- ◆ Planets
- ▲ A spacecraft
- ● A black hole

4 True or false: The arms of the Milky Way have names to identify them.
- ◆ True
- ▲ False

5 Where is the Solar System in the Milky Way?
- ◆ In the center
- ▲ On one of the smaller arms
- ● On one of the main arms

6 Which type of galaxy is the Milky Way?
- ◆ Elliptical
- ▲ Spiral
- ● Irregular
- ■ Peculiar

7 How old is the Milky Way?

◆ Hundreds of years

▲ Thousands of years

● Billions of years

8 What is the name of the group of galaxies that the Milky Way belongs to?

◆ Local Group

▲ Distant Group

● Invisible Group

Did you know?

Scientists believe that in 4 billion years the Milky Way and Andromeda galaxies will collide. The new galaxy will be called Milkomeda.

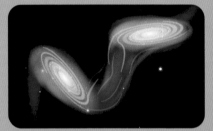

9 The Milky Way is measured in light years. How wide is it?

◆ 50,000 light years

▲ 120,000 light years

● 200,000 light years

Scan the QR code for a Kahoot! about the Milky Way.

10 Galaxies are held together by gravity. What is a group of galaxies called?

◆ A mass

▲ A swirl

● A cluster

Turn to page 32 for the answers!

Milky Way Answers

1 Put these in order from biggest to smallest:
- ▲ Universe
- ◆ Galaxy
- ● Solar System

The Universe contains billions of galaxies.

2 True or false: At night you can see the Milky Way?
- ◆ True

On a clear night, it looks like a band of milky light.

3 What is in the middle of the Milky Way?
- ● A black hole

At the very center of the Milky Way is a giant black hole that sucks in matter that gets too close.

4 True or false: The arms of the Milky Way have names to identify them.
- ◆ True

The two main arms are called Scutum-Centaurus and Perseus.

Scutum-Centaurus arm

Perseus arm

● Black hole

● Solar System

5 **Where is the Solar System in the Milky Way?**

▲ On one of the smaller arms

It is on the Orion Arm, which contains many of the brightest stars.

6 **Which type of galaxy is the Milky Way?**

▲ Spiral

The Milky Way has curved "arms" that spiral out from the center.

7 **How old is the Milky Way?**

● Billions of years

Our Solar System orbits the center of the Milky Way once every 225 million years.

8 **What is the name of the group of galaxies that the Milky Way belongs to?**

◆ Local Group

It includes three large spiral galaxies and 50 smaller galaxies.

9 **The Milky Way is measured in light years. How wide is it?**

▲ 120,000 light years

The widest galaxy is called IC 1101. It is an incredible 4 million light years wide.

10 **Galaxies are held together by gravity. What is a group of galaxies called?**

● A cluster

Galaxy clusters also contain hot gas and dark matter.

Podium!

Bronze: 1–5 correct answers

Silver: 6–8 correct answers

Gold: 9–10 correct answers

Satellites

Stop going round in circles, take a seat, and see how much satellite knowledge you have.

1 The two types of satellites are called . . .
- ◆ Big and small
- ▲ Natural and artificial
- ● Old and new

2 True or false: An artificial satellite is one made by humans.
- ◆ True
- ▲ False

4 Which of these is an artificial satellite?
- ◆ The International Space Station
- ▲ Lunar Rover
- ● Arecibo Observatory

5 Some artificial satellites are used for what?
- ◆ Waving to aliens
- ▲ Communication
- ● Finding lost pets

3 What do satellites use to power themselves?
- ◆ Rotating wheels
- ▲ Solar arrays
- ● Light from the Moon
- ■ Pedal power

6 Which country launched the first successful artificial satellite into space?
- ◆ United States
- ▲ France
- ● USSR

Did you know?

NASA has a fleet of 25 satellites orbiting and monitoring Earth. They record the quality of the air, weather patterns, and natural disasters. The satellites get data from remote parts of the world that cannot be reached any other way.

7 How long does it take most artificial satellites to orbit Earth?

◆ 2 hours
▲ 2 days
● 2 weeks

8 True or false: Padded jackets protect artificial satellites from extreme heat and cold.

◆ True
▲ False

9 When a satellite is preparing for launch it is known as . . .

◆ Luggage
▲ Payload
● Cargo

10 GPS uses a system of satellites. Where could you find one?

◆ In a computer
▲ In a vehicle
● In a shopping center

Turn to page 36 for the answers!

Satellites
Answers

1 The two types of satellites are called . . .
▲ Natural and artificial
A satellite is anything that orbits another body in space.

2 True or false: An artificial satellite is one made by humans.
◆ True
Natural satellites are objects made of natural materials, like the Moon.

3 What do satellites use to power themselves?
▲ Solar arrays
These are like large wings and are powered by the Sun.

4 Which of these is an artificial satellite?
◆ The International Space Station
Lunar Rovers are Moon-based space exploration vehicles and the Arecibo is an observatory in Puerto Rico.

5 Some artificial satellites are used for what?
▲ Communication
TV broadcasts and mobile phones use satellite signals.

6 Which country launched the first successful artificial satellite into space?

● USSR

Sputnik 1 was launched in 1957 from the country that is now Russia.

7 How long does it take most artificial satellites to orbit Earth?

◆ 2 hours

Most are in low orbit, which is 125–1,250 miles (200–2,000 km) above Earth's surface.

8 True or false: Padded jackets protect artificial satellites from extreme heat and cold.

▲ False

Insulating blankets that look like they are made of thin foil are used.

9 When a satellite is preparing for launch it is known as . . .

▲ Payload

A payload is the object a rocket carries into space.

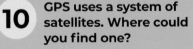

10 GPS uses a system of satellites. Where could you find one?

▲ In a vehicle

Sat-nav stands for satellite navigation and is used to provide vehicles with directions.

Podium!
Bronze: 1–5 correct answers
Silver: 6–8 correct answers
Gold: 9–10 correct answers

Black Holes

Dive into this quiz about black holes but don't get sucked into giving the wrong answers!

1 **What is the main force of a black hole?**
- ◆ Electricity
- ▲ The Sun's rays
- ● Gravity

2 **What causes a black hole?**
- ◆ Death of a star
- ▲ Planets colliding
- ● Satellite exploding

3 **True or false: There are tens of millions of black holes in the Milky Way.**
- ◆ True
- ▲ False

4 **What is the middle of a black hole called?**
- ◆ A singularity
- ▲ A pile
- ● A collection

5 **The smallest black holes are the size of what?**
- ◆ An atom
- ▲ An orange
- ● A football

6 What is a large black hole called?
- ◆ Supermassive
- ▲ Superhuge
- ● Supergigantic

7 The black hole at the center of our galaxy is called . . .
- ◆ Virgo A*
- ▲ Gemini A*
- ● Sagittarius A*

8 What does the energy from black holes power?
- ◆ The Sun
- ▲ Quasars
- ● Mars

9 Put these black holes in size order, starting with the smallest:
- ◆ Stellar
- ▲ Supermassive
- ● Primordial

10 If something is pulled into a black hole, can it escape?
- ◆ Depends on the size
- ▲ Never
- ● If it moves quickly

Scan the QR code for a Kahoot! about black holes.

Did you know?
Black holes are invisible, but telescopes can find them by observing what happens to the objects around them.

Turn to page 40 for the answers!

Black Holes
Answers

1 **What is the main force of a black hole?**
● Gravity
The pull of gravity is so strong that not even light can get out.

2 **What causes a black hole?**
◆ Death of a star
The dying star collapses under its own gravity.

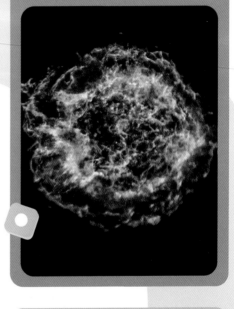

3 **True or false: There are tens of millions of black holes in the Milky Way.**
◆ True
Scientists think the nearest black hole is 1,500 light years away.

4 **What is the middle of a black hole called?**
◆ A singularity
The singularity is where matter is squashed to an unimaginably small point of infinite density. The outer edge of a black hole is called the event horizon.

5 **The smallest black holes are the size of what?**
◆ An atom
The smallest are called primordial black holes.

6 What is a large black hole called?

◆ Supermassive

There is a supermassive black hole at the center of the Milky Way.

7 The black hole at the center of our galaxy is called . . .

● Sagittarius A*

Its mass is equal to about 4 million Suns.

8 What does the energy from black holes power?

▲ Quasars

Quasars are a distant energy source that gives off radiation, like radio waves or X-rays.

9 Put these black holes in size order, starting with the smallest:

● Primordial

◆ Stellar

▲ Supermassive

What kind it is depends on the mass and size of the black hole.

10 If something is pulled into a black hole, can it escape?

▲ Never

Once an object has passed the event horizon at the edge of a black hole, it is lost forever.

Podium!

Bronze: 1–5 correct answers
Silver: 6–8 correct answers
Gold: 9–10 correct answers

Mercury

Can you keep up with speedy Mercury? See how fast you can complete this quiz.

1 **What is Mercury made of?**
- ◆ Gas and air
- ▲ Rock and metal
- ● Sand and ice

2 **How big is Mercury compared to Earth?**
- ◆ A third of the size
- ▲ Half the size
- ● Same size

3 **What is the temperature like on Mercury?**
- ◆ Always cold
- ▲ Always hot
- ● Hot during the day, cold at night

4 **How long does Mercury take to orbit the Sun?**
- ◆ 88 Earth months
- ▲ 88 Earth weeks
- ● 88 Earth days

5 **True or false: Mercury's orbit is elliptical, not circular.**
- ◆ True
- ▲ False

6 True or false: Mercury has two moons.

◆ True

▲ False

7 How long does it take Mercury to do one rotation?

◆ 12 Earth days

▲ 59 Earth days

● 98 Earth days

8 Put these planets in the order of how fast they orbit the Sun, from the fastest.

◆ Venus

▲ Mars

● Mercury

■ Earth

9 How long does a solar day take on Mercury?

◆ 12 Earth weeks

▲ 176 Earth days

● 5 Earth years

Did you know?

Mercury is not the hottest planet in the solar system—Venus is, due to its dense atmosphere.

10 Mercury is named after an ancient Roman god of . . .

◆ Speed

▲ Fire

● Shapeshifting

Turn to page 44 for the answers!

Mercury
Answers

1 **What is Mercury made of?**

▲ Rock and metal

Its core is made of iron and the mantle is silicate rock.

2 **How big is Mercury compared to Earth?**

◆ A third of the size

It has a radius of 1,516 miles (2,440 km).

EARTH

MERCURY

3 **What is the temperature like on Mercury?**

● Hot during the day, cold at night

It has no atmosphere to retain the heat from the Sun.

4 **How long does Mercury take to orbit the Sun?**

● 88 Earth days

This is exactly 50 percent longer than its rotation period.

5 **True or false: Mercury's orbit is elliptical, not circular.**

◆ True

It follows an oval pathway called an ellipse.

VENUS ●

● MERCURY

SUN

6 **True or false: Mercury has two moons.**

▲ False

The gravitational pull of the Sun would probably drag any satellite out of Mercury's orbit.

7 **How long does it take Mercury to do one rotation?**

▲ 59 Earth days

Its axis is only tilted by 2 degrees, so it spins nearly upright.

8 **Put these planets in the order of how fast they orbit the Sun, from the fastest.**

● Mercury (88 days)

◆ Venus (224 days),

■ Earth (365 days)

▲ Mars (686 days)

The closer a planet is to the Sun, the faster it travels.

9 **How long does a solar day take on Mercury?**

▲ 176 Earth days

A solar day lasts from one sunrise to the next.

10 **Mercury is named after an ancient Roman god of . . .**

◆ Speed

Mercury speeds around the Sun at 29 miles (47 km) per second, faster than any other planet.

Podium!

Bronze: 1–5 correct answers

Silver: 6–8 correct answers

Gold: 9–10 correct answers

Venus

Venus may be the Roman goddess of love, but the planet is toxic! Will you love this quiz or find it deadly?

1 **Venus is an . . .**
- ◆ Inner planet
- ▲ Outer planet
- ● Exoplanet

2 **What covers most of the surface of Venus?**
- ◆ Soot
- ▲ Chalk
- ● Volcanic rock

3 **How long is a year on Venus?**
- ◆ 5 Earth hours
- ▲ 225 Earth days
- ● 1 Earth year

4 **True or false: Venus is blanketed by a thick cloud of sulfuric acid.**
- ◆ True
- ▲ False

5 **What happened to the Magellan spacecraft after its mission to Venus in 1994?**
- ◆ It is still floating in space.
- ▲ It crashed into the surface.
- ● It burned up in the atmosphere.

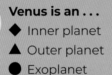

6 Put these Venus spacecraft in the order they launched.
- ◆ Mariner 2
- ▲ Akatsuki
- ● Galileo
- ■ Venus Express

7 True or false: The Maxwell Montes mountains on Venus are not as high as Mount Everest.
- ◆ True
- ▲ False

8 Venus has landscape features called . . .
- ◆ Pancake domes
- ▲ Muffin hills
- ● Pizza lakes

Did you know?
Radar orbiters are used to map the planet's surface because they can penetrate the thick clouds.

9 True or false: Venus spins in the opposite direction to the other planets.
- ◆ True
- ▲ False

10 How many rings does Venus have?
- ◆ None
- ▲ Two
- ● 27

Scan the QR code for a Kahoot! about Venus.

Turn to page 48 for the answers!

Venus
Answers

1 **Venus is an . . .**
◆ Inner planet
It is second closest to the Sun after Mercury.

2 **What covers most of the surface of Venus?**
● Volcanic rock
Venus has more than 1,600 volcanoes.

3 **How long is a year on Venus?**
▲ 225 Earth days
Its day is longer than its year at 243 Earth days. It spins backward, too!

4 **True or false: Venus is blanketed by a thick cloud of sulfuric acid.**
◆ True
The cloud stops sunlight reaching the surface.

5 **What happened to the Magellan spacecraft after its mission to Venus in 1994?**
● It burned up in the atmosphere.
This sounds dramatic, but it was the plan. Before that, it produced maps of the planet's surface.

Venus under the clouds

6 Put these Venus spacecraft in the order they launched.

◆ Mariner 2 (1962)
● Galileo (1990)
■ Venus Express (2005)
▲ Akatsuki (2010)

Mariner 2 was the first spacecraft to visit any planet from Earth.

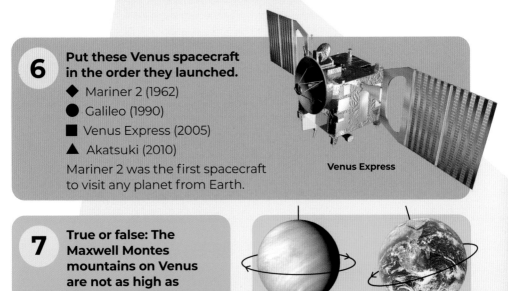

Venus Express

7 True or false: The Maxwell Montes mountains on Venus are not as high as Mount Everest.

▲ False

They are 7.5 miles (12 km) tall. Mount Everest is just 5.5 miles (8.8 km) tall.

Venus   **Earth**

8 Venus has landscape features called ...

◆ Pancake domes

These are volcanoes with flat tops and steep sides.

9 True or false: Venus spins in the opposite direction to the other planets.

◆ True

It spins counterclockwise. Watching from the surface, the Sun moves backward across the sky.

10 How many rings does Venus have?

◆ None

Venus is too close to the Sun to form the ice often found in planetary rings. As well as no rings, Venus also doesn't have any moons.

Podium!

Bronze: 1–5 correct answers
Silver: 6–8 correct answers
Gold: 9–10 correct answers

Earth

Get comfy—you should feel right at home as you tackle this down-to-earth quiz.

1 Most scientists believe life on Earth began where?
- ◆ In the air
- ▲ In the water
- ● On the land

2 Which gas makes up most of Earth's atmosphere?
- ◆ Oxygen
- ▲ Nitrogen
- ● Carbon dioxide

3 How long does it take for Earth to go around the Sun?
- ◆ 1 day
- ▲ 7 days
- ● 365 days

4 What is the first layer of the solid surface of Earth called?
- ◆ Mantle
- ▲ Crust
- ● Atmosphere

5 True or false: The temperature at Earth's core is hotter than the Sun's surface.
- ◆ True
- ▲ False

6 Which continent does this show?

◆ Europe
▲ Africa
● South America

7 True or false: Earth's atmosphere is warming up because heat is being trapped on Earth's surface.

◆ True
▲ False

8 Put the four major outer layers of Earth's atmosphere in order from top to bottom . . .

◆ Mesosphere
▲ Stratosphere
● Exosphere
■ Thermosphere

Did you know?

All of the planets are named after Greek and Roman gods and goddesses except Earth, which is from a Germanic word meaning "the ground."

9 How much have sea levels risen since 1992?

◆ 1 in (2.5 cm)
▲ 2 in (5 cm)
● 3 in (7.6 cm)
■ 5 in (12.7 cm)

10 How much of Earth's surface is covered by water?

◆ Half
▲ Three-quarters
● Two-thirds

Turn to page 52 for the answers!

Earth

Answers

1 Most scientists believe life on Earth began where?

▲ In the water

Water is vital to all life forms on Earth.

2 Which gas makes up most of Earth's atmosphere?

▲ Nitrogen

About 78 percent of Earth's air is nitrogen.

3 How long does it take for Earth to go around the Sun?

● 365 days

As Earth moves, its changing tilt relative to the Sun produces the seasons.

4 What is the first layer of the solid surface of Earth called?

▲ Crust

It is only a few tens of miles thick.

5 True or false: The temperature at Earth's core is hotter than the Sun's surface.

◆ True

Temperatures at Earth's core can be 10,800°F (6,000°C). The Sun's surface only reaches 10,000°F (5,500°C).

6 **Which continent does this show?**

▲ Africa

This is one of the seven large land masses on Earth called continents.

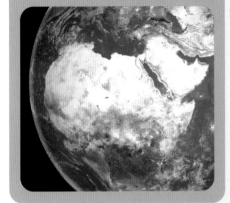

7 **True or false: Earth's atmosphere is warming up because heat is being trapped on Earth's surface.**

◆ True

This is the Greenhouse Effect and it's caused by the burning of fossil fuels, such as coal, oil, and natural gas.

8 **Put the four major outer layers of Earth's atmosphere in order from top to bottom . . .**

● Exosphere

■ Thermosphere

◆ Mesosphere

▲ Stratosphere

The very bottom layer is the Troposphere.

9 **How much have sea levels risen since 1992?**

● 3 in (7.6 cm)

The Greenland ice sheet is pouring about 330 billion tons of ice a year into the ocean as it melts.

Podium!

Bronze: 1–5 correct answers

Silver: 6–8 correct answers

Gold: 9–10 correct answers

10 **How much of Earth's surface is covered by water?**

● Two-thirds

About 97 percent of the water is found in the oceans.

Mars

Don't see red doing this quiz.
Make sure you have all the Mars
knowledge you need.

1 Why is Mars known as
the Red Planet?
- ◆ It's covered in red dust.
- ▲ Its atmosphere is red.
- ● It's covered in
  red algae.

2 True or false:
Mars has seasons
like Earth.
- ◆ True
- ▲ False

3 What is the
Olympus Mons on Mars?
- ◆ Crater
- ▲ Volcano
- ● Sea

4 Mars has giant valleys
made by . . .
- ◆ Forests
- ▲ Rivers
- ● Continents

5 How many moons
does Mars have?
- ◆ 1
- ▲ 2
- ● 3

6 True or false: It takes over a year to reach Mars from Earth.
- ◆ True
- ▲ False

7 How long does it take Mars to make one rotation?
- ◆ 25 hours
- ▲ 4 days
- ● 12 days
- ■ 28 days

Insight

8 Put these Mars exploration craft in order from the earliest . . .
- ◆ Curiosity
- ▲ Insight
- ● Perseverance
- ■ Opportunity

Did you know?
Some scientists believe humans could live on Mars if they could find a way to protect people from the fierce radiation.

9 What happened to the Deep Space 2 probe sent to Mars in 1999?
- ◆ Still on Mars
- ▲ Lost in space
- ● Exploded in space

10 True or false: Mars has had more space probes than any other planet.
- ◆ True
- ▲ False

Scan the QR code for a Kahoot! about Mars.

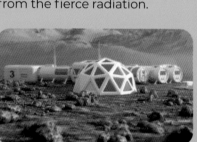

Turn to page 56 for the answers!

Mars Answers

1. Why is Mars known as the Red Planet?

◆ It's covered in red dust.

This is caused by iron minerals rusting.

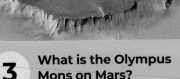

3. What is the Olympus Mons on Mars?

▲ Volcano

It is the largest in the Solar System at 374 miles (624 km) across and 16 miles (25 km) high.

2. True or false: Mars has seasons like Earth.

◆ True

But they are all freezing cold and dry as Mars has no rain.

4. Mars has giant valleys made by . . .

▲ Rivers

These valleys have been preserved after being formed by rivers billions of years ago.

5 How many moons does Mars have?

▲ 2

Phobos and Deimos are named after Greek gods.

6 True or false: It takes over a year to reach Mars from Earth.

▲ False

It takes 150 to 300 days.

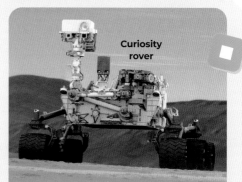

Curiosity rover

7 How long does it take Mars to make one rotation?

◆ 25 hours

Due to the time it takes to complete one rotation, a day on Mars (25 hours) is similar in length to a day on Earth (24 hours).

8 Put these Mars exploration craft in order from the earliest . . .

■ Opportunity (2004)

◆ Curiosity (2012)

▲ Insight (2018)

● Perseverance (2021)

Opportunity roamed Mars for almost 15 years.

9 What happened to the Deep Space 2 probe sent to Mars in 1999?

▲ Lost in space

It arrived on Mars, then all contact was lost.

Podium!

Bronze: 1–5 correct answers
Silver: 6–8 correct answers
Gold: 9–10 correct answers

10 True or false: Mars has had more space probes than any other planet.

◆ True

Mars is nicknamed the "spacecraft graveyard" because of how many probes have failed.

Jupiter

Stop mooning about and take a peek at this quiz about Jupiter and its many moons.

1 True or false: Jupiter is the second biggest planet.
- ◆ True
- ▲ False

2 How many moons does Jupiter have?
- ◆ 29
- ▲ 59
- ● 80

3 How long does it take Jupiter to complete one rotation?
- ◆ 5 hours
- ▲ 10 hours
- ● 3 days

4 What are Jupiter's first four moons called?
- ◆ Galilean satellites
- ▲ Copernicus satellites
- ● Hubble satellites

5 How long is Jupiter's year?
- ◆ 6 Earth years
- ▲ 12 Earth years
- ● 24 Earth years

6 Which of Jupiter's moons is the largest in the Solar System?

◆ Metis

▲ Ganymede

● Thebe

■ Io

7 Put the Galilean moons in order from Jupiter outward.

◆ Callisto

▲ Io

● Europa

■ Ganymede

Did you know?

Jupiter's moon Ganymede is 10 percent wider than Mercury and would be called a planet if it orbited the Sun.

8 Which is the main gas that makes up Jupiter's atmosphere?

◆ Helium

▲ Oxygen

● Hydrogen

■ Carbon dioxide

9 What is the Great Red Spot on Jupiter?

◆ A massive storm

▲ A huge pimple

● A vast lava lake

10 True or false: Jupiter is an exoplanet because it orbits the Sun.

◆ True

▲ False

Turn to page 60 for the answers!

Jupiter Answers

1 **True or false: Jupiter is the second biggest planet.**
▲ False
Jupiter is the biggest planet. It's almost twice the size of all the other planets put together!

2 **How many moons does Jupiter have?**
● 80
57 have been named, including Praxidike, Themisto, and Dia.

3 **How long does it take Jupiter to complete one rotation?**
▲ 10 hours
It's the fastest-spinning planet.

4 **What are Jupiter's first four moons called?**
◆ Galilean satellites
They are named after an Italian astronomer, Galileo, who discovered them in 1610.

5 **How long is Jupiter's year?**
▲ 12 Earth years
It orbits five times farther from the Sun than Earth.

6 Which of Jupiter's moons is the largest in the Solar System?

▲ Ganymede

It lies 665,000 miles (1.07 million km) from Jupiter.

7 Put the Galilean moons in order from Jupiter outward.

▲ Io
● Europa
■ Ganymede
◆ Callisto

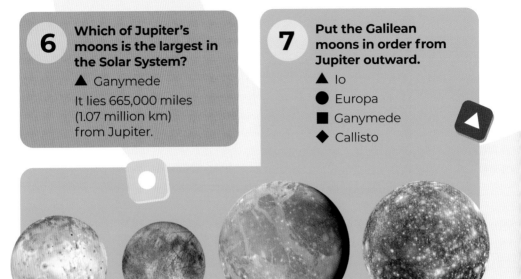

IO   EUROPA   GANYMEDE   CALLISTO

8 Which is the main gas that makes up Jupiter's atmosphere?

● Hydrogen

It makes up 90 percent of the atmosphere; the rest is mainly helium.

9 What is the Great Red Spot on Jupiter?

◆ A massive storm

It is so large that two Earths could fit inside it.

Podium!

Bronze: 1–5 correct answers
Silver: 6–8 correct answers
Gold: 9–10 correct answers

10 True or false: Jupiter is an exoplanet because it orbits the Sun.

▲ False

Exoplanets are planets that orbit stars outside of our solar system.

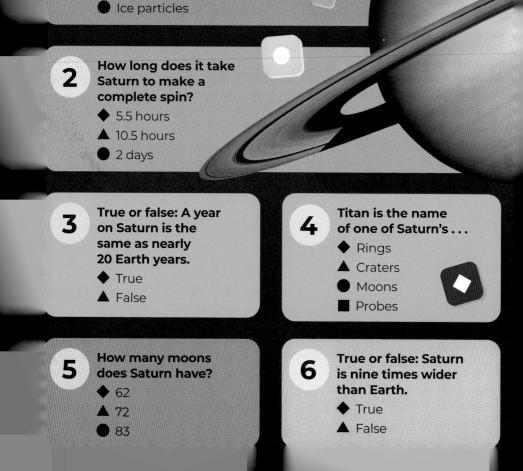

Saturn

Don't get in a spin and let this quiz run rings round you. Brush up on your Saturn knowledge.

1 What are Saturn's rings made of?
- ◆ Tiny rocks
- ▲ Stars
- ● Ice particles

2 How long does it take Saturn to make a complete spin?
- ◆ 5.5 hours
- ▲ 10.5 hours
- ● 2 days

3 True or false: A year on Saturn is the same as nearly 20 Earth years.
- ◆ True
- ▲ False

4 Titan is the name of one of Saturn's . . .
- ◆ Rings
- ▲ Craters
- ● Moons
- ■ Probes

5 How many moons does Saturn have?
- ◆ 62
- ▲ 72
- ● 83

6 True or false: Saturn is nine times wider than Earth.
- ◆ True
- ▲ False

7 What do Saturn's moons Epimetheus and Janus do every four years?
- ◆ Collide
- ▲ Grow bigger
- ● Swap orbits

8 Put these moons in the order of how close they are to Saturn.
- ◆ Rhea
- ▲ Titan
- ● Atlas
- ■ Calypso

Did you know?

Saturn's rings are made of billions of fragments of ice. Some are as big as icebergs. Gravity has pulled the material in Saturn's rings into a thin disc.

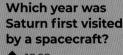

9 Which year was Saturn first visited by a spacecraft?
- ◆ 1969
- ▲ 1979
- ● 2009

Scan the QR code for a Kahoot! about Saturn.

10 How many planets away from the Sun is Saturn?
- ◆ Six
- ▲ Seven
- ● Eight

Turn to page 64 for the answers!

Saturn
Answers

1 **What are Saturn's rings made of?**

● Ice particles

They look very bright when the ice reflects the Sun.

2 **How long does it take Saturn to make a complete spin?**

▲ 10.5 hours

It has the second shortest day in the Solar System after Jupiter.

4 **Titan is the name of one of Saturn's . . .**

● Moons

It is Saturn's largest moon, with a diameter of 3,200 miles (5,150 km).

3 **True or false: A year on Saturn is the same as nearly 20 Earth years.**

▲ False

A year on Saturn is 29.5 Earth years.

5 How many moons does Saturn have?
● 83
Of these, 20 are still waiting to be named.

6 True or false: Saturn is nine times wider than Earth.
◆ True
Saturn has a diameter of 72,365 miles (116,460 km).

7 What do Saturn's moons Epimetheus and Janus do every four years?
● Swap orbits
They are so close together, their gravity makes them swap orbital paths.

8 Put these moons in the order of how close they are to Saturn.
● Atlas
■ Calypso
◆ Rhea
▲ Titan
Rhea is Saturn's second-largest moon.

9 Which year was Saturn first visited by a spacecraft?
▲ 1979
It was visited by NASA's Pioneer 11.

10 How many planets away from the Sun is Saturn?
◆ Six
It is one of the four large outer planets.

Podium!
Bronze: 1–5 correct answers
Silver: 6–8 correct answers
Gold: 9–10 correct answers

Uranus

Be cool, not blue, as you race through this quiz and get as many questions correct as you can.

1 **What color is Uranus?**
◆ Red
▲ Yellow
● Blue

2 **How long is a year on Uranus?**
◆ 26 Earth years
▲ 48 Earth years
● 84 Earth years

3 **True or false: Uranus spins totally upright.**
◆ True
▲ False

4 **Which astronomer discovered Uranus?**
◆ Galileo
▲ William Herschel
● Copernicus
■ Edwin Hubble

5 **Which is Uranus's largest moon?**
◆ Juliet
▲ Titania
● Desdemona
■ Cordelia

6 How many rings does Uranus have?
◆ 3
▲ 13
● 23

7 Which is the only spacecraft sent to Uranus?
◆ Voyager 2
▲ Perseverance
● Explorer 1

8 True or false: It takes sunlight 24 Earth days to travel to Uranus.
◆ True
▲ False

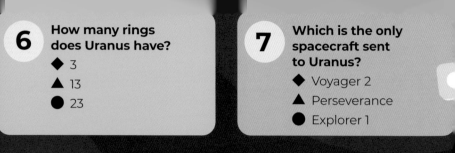

Did you know?
Many of Uranus's moons are named after characters from Shakespeare's plays.

9 What kind of planet is Uranus?
◆ An ice giant
▲ A gas giant
● A wood giant
■ A rocky giant

10 Uranus is one of the four outer planets. Put them in order from the Sun.
◆ Neptune
▲ Jupiter
● Uranus
■ Saturn

Turn to page 68 for the answers!

Uranus
Answers

1 **What color is Uranus?**
● Blue
This is caused by methane gas in its atmosphere.

2 **How long is a year on Uranus?**
● 84 Earth years
It takes 17.2 hours to make one rotation.

3 **True or false: Uranus spins totally upright.**
▲ False
It is the only planet to spin on its side.

4 **Which astronomer discovered Uranus?**
▲ William Herschel
He discovered it in 1781 in his garden using a homemade telescope.

5 Which is Uranus's largest moon?

▲ Titania

It is 980 miles (1,577 km) wide.

6 How many rings does Uranus have?

▲ 13

The first were discovered in 1977.

7 Which is the only spacecraft sent to Uranus?

◆ Voyager 2

In 1986, it discovered 10 previously unknown moons.

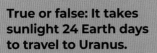

8 True or false: It takes sunlight 24 Earth days to travel to Uranus.

▲ False

It only takes 2 hours and 40 minutes for sunlight to reach Uranus.

9 What kind of planet is Uranus?

◆ An ice giant

It is mostly made of flowing icy materials with an atmosphere of methane, hydrogen, and helium.

10 Uranus is one of the four outer planets. Put them in order from the Sun.

▲ Jupiter

■ Saturn

● Uranus

◆ Neptune

Beyond Neptune lies the Kuiper Belt.

Podium!

Bronze: 1–5 correct answers
Silver: 6–8 correct answers
Gold: 9–10 correct answers

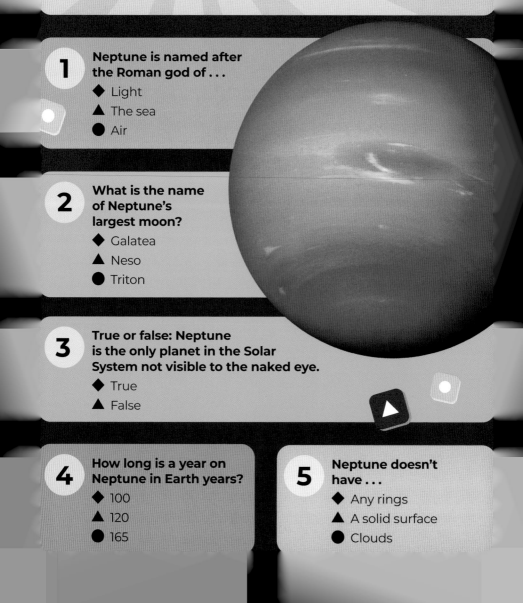

Neptune

Sharpen your wits and your pencils to come out triumphant in this quiz.

1 Neptune is named after the Roman god of . . .
- ◆ Light
- ▲ The sea
- ● Air

2 What is the name of Neptune's largest moon?
- ◆ Galatea
- ▲ Neso
- ● Triton

3 True or false: Neptune is the only planet in the Solar System not visible to the naked eye.
- ◆ True
- ▲ False

4 How long is a year on Neptune in Earth years?
- ◆ 100
- ▲ 120
- ● 165

5 Neptune doesn't have . . .
- ◆ Any rings
- ▲ A solid surface
- ● Clouds

6 Put these Neptune moons in order of size, starting with the largest.

◆ Sao
▲ Larissa
● Galatea
■ Nereid

7 True or false: Neptune has an icy sea under its surface.

◆ True
▲ False

8 What is Neptune's weather like?

◆ Very windy
▲ Very calm
● Very mild

9 How far is Neptune from the Sun in Astronomical Units?

◆ 10
▲ 20
● 30

10 How many moons does Neptune have?

◆ 10
▲ 12
● 14

Did you know?

One of Neptune's moons, Triton, is the only large moon in the Solar System that circles its planet in the opposite direction to the planet's rotation.

Scan the QR code for a Kahoot! about Neptune.

Turn to page 72 for the answers!

Neptune
Answers

1 **Neptune is named after the Roman god of . . .**
▲ The sea

Urbain Le Verrier suggested the name. His mathematical calculations helped Johann Gottfried Galle discover the planet.

2 **What is the name of Neptune's largest moon?**
● Triton

It is almost four fifths as wide as Earth's Moon at 1,680 miles (2,700 km) in diameter.

Triton   Moon

3 **True or false: Neptune is the only planet in the Solar System not visible to the naked eye.**
◆ True

It is the only planet to be discovered by mathematical calculations.

4 **How long is a year on Neptune in Earth years?**
● 165

Because its year is so long, each season lasts for more than 40 years.

5 Neptune doesn't have . . .
▲ A solid surface

It has a very deep atmosphere that melts into water.

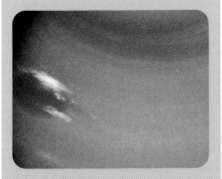

Neptune's blue color comes from methane in its atmosphere.

6 Put these Neptune moons in order of size, starting with the largest.
■ Nereid
▲ Larissa
● Galatea
◆ Sao

Neptune has 14 moons in total.

7 True or false: Neptune has an icy sea under its surface.
▲ False

Scientists believe the ocean is extremely hot.

8 What is Neptune's weather like?
◆ Very windy

Wind speed can reach up to 1,300 mph (2,100 kph).

9 How far is Neptune from the Sun in Astronomical Units?
● 30

An Astronomical Unit (AU) is the distance from Earth to the Sun.

10 How many moons does Neptune have?
● 14

Many were discovered by Voyager 2 in 1989. The tiny Neptune moon, Hippocamp, was discovered in 2013.

Podium!

Bronze: 1–5 correct answers
Silver: 6–8 correct answers
Gold: 9–10 correct answers

Pluto

It may be a small planet, but this quiz is just as big as the others. Aim for the stars!

1 What type of planet is Pluto?
- ◆ Major planet
- ▲ Dwarf planet
- ● Exoplanet

2 Pluto has . . .
- ◆ Moons but no rings
- ▲ Rings but no moons
- ● No rings or moons

3 What is the name of Pluto's biggest moon?
- ◆ Hydra
- ▲ Nix
- ● Charon
- ■ Styx

4 How many Earth years does it take for Pluto to orbit the Sun?
- ◆ 6
- ▲ 124
- ● 248

5 True or false: Pluto is part of a group of icy objects called the Kuiper Belt.
- ◆ True
- ▲ False

6 **What is Pluto also known as?**
- ◆ Prince Pluto
- ▲ King of the Kuiper Belt
- ● Count Planet

Charon

Did you know?

Pluto was discovered by Clyde Tombaugh in 1930. He once said he wanted to visit the planet. In 2006 his ashes were placed onboard the New Horizons probe. In 2015 it came within 7,500 miles (12,070 km) of Pluto.

7 **Put these four moons in order, starting with the nearest to Pluto.**
- ◆ Kerberos
- ▲ Styx
- ● Nix
- ■ Charon

8 **True or false: Pluto is only half as wide as the United States.**
- ◆ True
- ▲ False

9 **Pluto travels round the Sun in what kind of orbit?**
- ◆ An oval orbit
- ▲ A circular orbit
- ● A square orbit

10 **When did the New Horizons spacecraft pass by Pluto?**
- ◆ 2000
- ▲ 2015
- ● 2020

Turn to page 76 for the answers!

Pluto
Answers

1 **What type of planet is Pluto?**
▲ Dwarf planet
This means it's not big enough to have cleared the area around its orbit.

2 **Pluto has . . .**
◆ Moons but no rings
It has five moons in total: Charon, Hydra, Styx, Nix, and Kerberos.

3 **What is the name of Pluto's biggest moon?**
● Charon
It is so big, it's about half the size of Pluto.

4 **How many Earth years does it take for Pluto to orbit the Sun?**
● 248
Its day lasts for 153 hours.

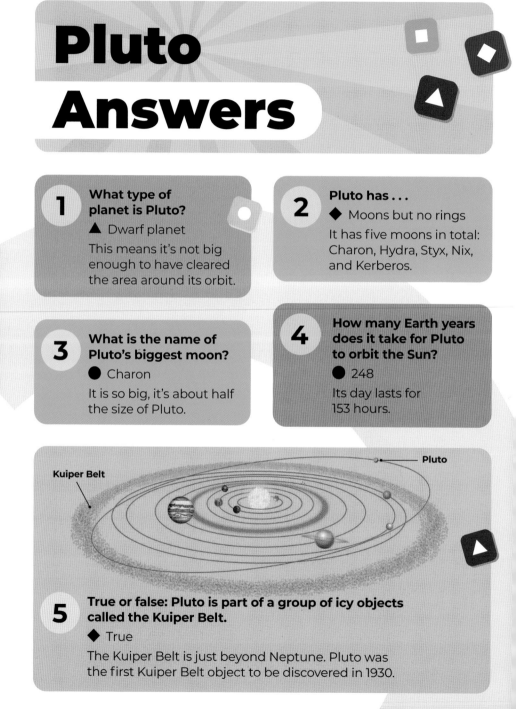

Pluto

Kuiper Belt

5 **True or false: Pluto is part of a group of icy objects called the Kuiper Belt.**
◆ True
The Kuiper Belt is just beyond Neptune. Pluto was the first Kuiper Belt object to be discovered in 1930.

6 **What is Pluto also known as?**

▲ King of the Kuiper Belt

Pluto is the biggest object in the Kuiper Belt, hence the name.

7 **Put these four moons in order, starting with the nearest to Pluto.**

■ Charon

▲ Styx

● Nix

◆ Kerberos

Pluto's moon system is thought to be a result of a collision between Pluto and another Kuiper Belt object. The fifth and furthest moon is Hydra.

8 **True or false: Pluto is only half as wide as the United States.**

◆ True

Pluto is about 1,480 miles (2,380 km) wide.

9 **Pluto travels round the Sun in what kind of orbit?**

◆ An oval orbit

Most planets have a more circular orbit.

10 **When did the New Horizons spacecraft pass by Pluto?**

▲ 2015

It is the only spacecraft to have passed by Pluto, and it took nearly 10 years to get there.

Podium!

Bronze: 1–5 correct answers

Silver: 6–8 correct answers

Gold: 9–10 correct answers

Sun

Don't get hot and bothered with this dazzling quiz. Brighten up . . . it's time to shine!

1 What is the Sun?
- ◆ A star
- ▲ A planet
- ● A meteorite

2 What keeps other objects orbiting the Sun?
- ◆ Solar power
- ▲ Gravity
- ● The Moon

3 True or false: The Sun is the biggest object in the Solar System.
- ◆ True
- ▲ False

4 The surface of the Sun consists of . . .
- ◆ Boiling water
- ▲ Plasma
- ● Rock

5 What are the dark patches on the Sun called?
- ◆ Sunspots
- ▲ Hotspots
- ● Black spots
- ■ Spots

6 True or false: A solar flare can affect radio communications on Earth.
- ◆ True
- ▲ False

7 Where is the Sun's corona?
- ◆ At its core
- ▲ At the outermost part of its atmosphere
- ● Floating around it

8 The size of our Sun compared to other stars in the Milky Way is . . .
- ◆ Big
- ▲ Small
- ● Average

9 Because of its age, our Sun is currently . . .
- ◆ A yellow dwarf
- ▲ A white dwarf
- ● A red giant

10 What is a solar eclipse?
- ◆ When a cloud hides the Sun
- ▲ When the Moon passes between the Sun and Earth
- ● When Mercury passes in front of the Sun

Did you know?
The Sun is 4.5 billion years old. In another few billion years it will turn into a red giant and later a white dwarf.

Scan the QR code for a Kahoot! about the Sun.

Turn to page 80 for

Sun

Answers

1 **What is the Sun?**
◆ A star
The Sun is the only star in our Solar System, and other objects orbit around it.

2 **What keeps other objects orbiting the Sun?**
▲ Gravity
This is an invisible force. The more mass an object has, the stronger its gravity.

3 **True or false: The Sun is the biggest object in the Solar System.**
◆ True
It contains 99.8 percent of the Solar System's entire mass.

4 **The surface of the Sun consists of . . .**
▲ Plasma
This is a mix of super-hot glowing gases, mainly helium and hydrogen.

5 **What are the dark patches on the Sun called?**
◆ Sunspots
Sunspots look dark because they are 3,600°F (2,000°C) cooler than the rest of the surface.

Sunspots

6 **True or false: A solar flare can affect radio communications on Earth.**

◆ True

Solar flares are sudden explosions of energy that send radiation into space.

Solar Flare

7 **Where is the Sun's corona?**

▲ At the outermost part of its atmosphere

It's only visible during a total solar eclipse. Never ever look directly at the Sun—it can damage your eyes.

Corona

8 **The size of our Sun compared to other stars in the Milky Way is . . .**

● Average

Stars vary in size. Some are 100 times bigger and some a tenth of the size of our Sun.

9 **Because of its age, our Sun is currently . . .**

◆ A yellow dwarf

At four-and-a-half billion years old, the Sun is halfway through its life cycle.

10 **What is a solar eclipse?**

▲ When the Moon passes between the Sun and Earth

Although the Moon is much smaller than the Sun, it is so much closer to us that it can block out the Sun's disc in our skies.

Podium!

Bronze: 1–5 correct answers
Silver: 6–8 correct answers
Gold: 9–10 correct answers

Rockets

This quiz isn't a walk in the park . . . well, it is rocket science after all.

1 Rocket engines burn fuel and turn it into . . .
◆ Hot gas
▲ Oxygen
● Food

2 How much fuel does a rocket burn every second?
◆ 5.5 tons (5 tonnes)
▲ 11 tons (10 tonnes)
● 16.5 tons (15 tonnes)
■ 22 tons (20 tonnes)

3 Why are rockets made from titanium or aluminum?
◆ They need to be shiny to glow in the night sky.
▲ These metals are cheap.
● These metals are smooth.
■ They must be lightweight but strong.

4 What is the force that pushes a rocket called?
◆ Electric
▲ Magnetic
● Trust
■ Thrust

5 What were the first rockets invented used for?
◆ Fireworks
▲ Weapons
● Space exploration

6 Where do rocket engines go when they burn up all their fuel?

- ◆ They separate from the rocket.
- ▲ They stay still until they can be refilled.
- ● They turn into extra propellers.
- ■ They shrivel up.

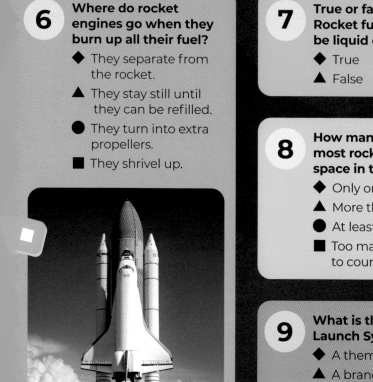

Did you know?

It would take 500,000 cars to generate the same amount of power as NASA's newest rocket at lift off.

7 True or false: Rocket fuel can be liquid or solid.

- ◆ True
- ▲ False

8 How many times do most rockets fly to space in their lifetime?

- ◆ Only once
- ▲ More than 5 times
- ● At least 20 times
- ■ Too many times to count

9 What is the Space Launch System (SLS)?

- ◆ A theme park ride
- ▲ A brand-new space center
- ● NASA's giant new rocket

10 Which is the only part of a rocket that returns to Earth after flight?

- ◆ Wings
- ▲ Fuel tanks
- ● Crew module
- ■ Boosters

Turn to page 84 for the answers!

Rockets
Answers

1 Rocket engines burn fuel and turn it into . . .

◆ Hot gas

The engine contains fuel and a chemical called oxidizer. When ignited, they react to create hot gas.

2 How much fuel does a rocket burn every second?

● 16.5 tons (15 tonnes)

A rocket's weight is mainly made up of fuel. Almost all of a rocket's fuel is used up in the first few minutes.

3 Why are rockets made from titanium or aluminum?

■ They must be lightweight but strong.

Just like the frame of an airplane, a rocket needs to be made of material that won't slow it down or fall apart.

4 What is the force that pushes a rocket called?

■ Thrust

To reach orbit, a rocket needs enough thrust to reach a speed of 17,500 mph (28,000 kph). That's faster than the speed of sound, which is 767 mph (1,235 kph)!

5 What were the first rockets invented used for?

◆ Fireworks

The first known rockets were invented in China in the 1200s. Armies then also used them in wars.

6 Where do rocket engines go when they burn up all their fuel?

◆ They separate from the rocket.

As each engine runs out of fuel, it detaches and either falls into the ocean or stays in space.

7 True or false: Rocket fuel can be liquid or solid.

◆ True

Some rockets use both in different sections called stages.

8 How many times do most rockets fly to space in their lifetime?

◆ Only once

Most rockets are built to make just one journey, but reusable ones are becoming more common.

9 What is the Space Launch System (SLS)?

● NASA's giant new rocket

The SLS is the most powerful rocket ever built by NASA. It will be able to take astronauts further into space than ever before.

10 Which is the only part of a rocket that returns to Earth after flight?

● Crew module

For a successful flight, the crew module is the most important part of a rocket and must land safely. Parachutes are usually used to ensure a soft landing.

Podium!

Bronze: 1–5 correct answers
Silver: 6–8 correct answers
Gold: 9–10 correct answers

International Space Station

Test your knowledge of humanity's record-breaking outpost in space.

1 What is the International Space Station (ISS) for?
- ◆ A place to get away from crowds
- ▲ A high-security space prison
- ● A long-term base for observing Earth and space

2 How many space stations are in orbit right now?
- ◆ 1
- ▲ 2
- ● 10

3 When was the first module of the ISS launched?
- ◆ 1978
- ▲ 1988
- ● 1998

4 Why are tape and Velcro™ essential at an astronaut's desk?
- ◆ For arts and crafts activities
- ▲ To stop their pens and paper floating away
- ● As decoration

5 True or false: The ISS is visible from Earth.
- ◆ True
- ▲ False

6 How does the ISS stay up in space?

◆ It's so lightweight that it floats.

▲ It attaches itself to planets and stars.

● It travels at a high rate of speed.

7 How long does it take for the ISS to orbit Earth once?

◆ About 30 minutes

▲ About 90 minutes

● More than one day

■ More than three days

8 How many people live aboard the ISS at one time?

◆ 3

▲ 7

● 15

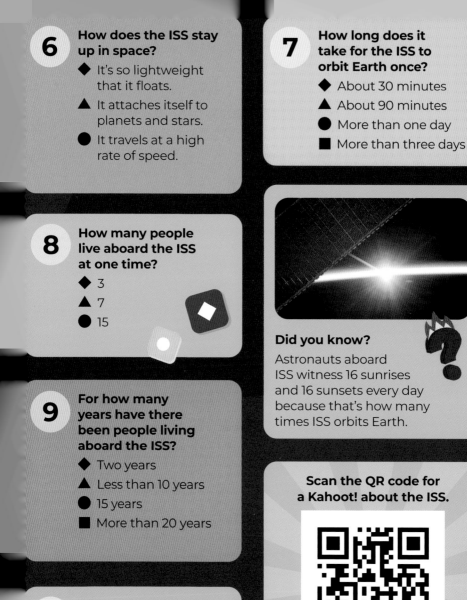

Did you know?

Astronauts aboard ISS witness 16 sunrises and 16 sunsets every day because that's how many times ISS orbits Earth.

9 For how many years have there been people living aboard the ISS?

◆ Two years

▲ Less than 10 years

● 15 years

■ More than 20 years

Scan the QR code for a Kahoot! about the ISS.

Turn to page 88 for the answers!

10 True or false: The ISS relies on burning coal to power its electricity.

◆ True

▲ False

International Space Station

Answers

1 **What is the International Space Station (ISS) for?**

● A long-term base for observing Earth and space

The International Space Station is a laboratory for people to live and work in.

2 **How many space stations are in orbit right now?**

▲ 2

China's Tiangong space station and the ISS are both in orbit.

3 **When was the first module of the ISS launched?**

● 1998

It wasn't as big in 1998— more modules have been added since then.

4 **Why are tape and Velcro™ essential at an astronaut's desk?**

▲ To stop their pens and paper floating away

Items can be stored on the desk, walls, or ceiling to save space, so long as they're secured in place.

5 **True or false: The ISS is visible from Earth.**

◆ True

At night, you can see the International Space Station without a telescope. There are even tracking apps that can tell you when it's passing where you live.

6 How does the ISS stay up in space?
● It travels at a high rate of speed.
The ISS is in orbit, which means its high speed balances out the pull of Earth's gravity.

7 How long does it take for the ISS to orbit Earth once?
▲ About 90 minutes
Travelling at a speed of 17,500 mph (28,000 kph), the space station is kept going by space agencies of Russia, the United States, Canada, Europe, and Japan.

8 How many people live aboard the ISS at one time?
▲ 7
A crew of seven specially selected and highly trained international astronauts usually live aboard the ISS.

9 For how many years have there been people living aboard the ISS?
■ More than 20 years
The space station has been lived on continuously since November 2000.

10 True or false: The ISS relies on burning coal to power its electricity.
▲ False
Solar power is used to supply the space station with electricity. It has enormous solar panels to soak up the sunlight.

Podium!
Bronze: 1–5 correct answers
Silver: 6–8 correct answers
Gold: 9–10 correct answers

Robots and Probes

These probing questions are sure to get your brain spinning . . .

1 **Why do astronauts need robots?**
- ◆ For company
- ▲ To cook
- ● To help with many tasks, especially dangerous ones

2 **Robonaut 2 is a humanoid robot. This means . . .**
- ◆ It can think
- ▲ It has emotions
- ● It has a human shape

3 **True or false: Robonaut 2's "brains" are positioned where its stomach would be.**
- ◆ True
- ▲ False

4 **What is Dextre?**
- ◆ A small round robot
- ▲ A two-armed robot
- ● A robot on wheels

5 **Dextre was built by which space agency?**
- ◆ Russian
- ▲ Canadian
- ● Chinese

6 Voyager 1 is the first human-made object to travel furthest into space. Where did it reach?

◆ Pluto
▲ The Kuiper Belt
● The heliosphere

7 What is special about the robot BRUIE?

◆ It can talk.
▲ It can withstand the Sun's heat.
● It can travel along the underside of ice.
■ It can contact aliens.

8 Put these space probes in order from oldest to newest.

◆ Lucy
▲ Sputnik
● Mariner 2
■ Parker Solar Probe

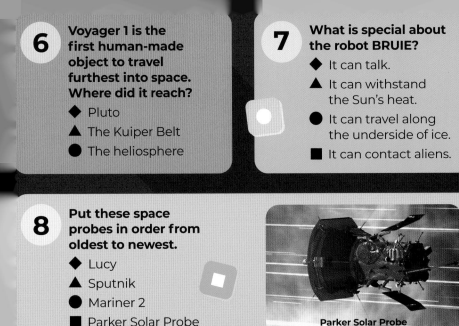

Parker Solar Probe

Did you know?

The Astrobees are three cube-shaped robots named Bumble, Honey, and Queen. They help astronauts with everyday tasks such as monitoring air levels, and each is activated when it hears its name.

9 What do space probes Voyager 1 and 2 carry?

◆ Games consoles from the 1990s
▲ DNA samples from every animal species
● Messages for aliens
■ A range of chocolate bars from around the world

10 True or false: Mariner 4 was the first probe to take a picture of Mars?

◆ True
▲ False

Turn to page 92 for the answers!

Robots and Probes

Answers

1 Why do astronauts need robots?
● To help with many tasks, especially dangerous ones
Robots carry out all sorts of tasks, but especially those that are risky, repetitive, or need additional tools.

2 Robonaut 2 is a humanoid robot. This means . . .
● It has a human shape
To begin with, it was mounted on a platform. Legs were attached to its body three years later so it could move around and do more tasks.

3 True or false: Robonaut 2's "brains" are positioned where its stomach would be.
◆ True
This is where its computers were loaded. It is faster than Robonaut 1 (which never left Earth) and its hands work just like human hands.

4 What is Dextre?
▲ A two-armed robot
Also known as the Special Purpose Dexterous Manipulator (SPDM), it is part of the ISS and mainly does electrical repairs outside the spacecraft.

5 Dextre was built by which space agency?
▲ Canadian
Dextre is controlled from the ground at Houston, Texas, which frees the ISS crew to do other tasks.

6 Voyager 1 is the first human-made object to travel furthest into space. Where did it reach?

● The heliosphere

The heliosphere is the outer edge of the Solar System.

7 What is special about the robot BRUIE?

● It can travel along the underside of ice.

BRUIE stands for Buoyant Rover for Under-Ice Exploration. It can float and take pictures and other data in ice-covered seas.

8 Put these space probes in order from oldest to newest.

▲ Sputnik (1957)

● Mariner 2 (1962)

■ Parker Solar Probe (2018)

◆ Lucy (2021)

9 What do space probes Voyager 1 and 2 carry?

● Messages for aliens

They carry a message saying they are from Earth plus pictures, music, and greetings in 55 languages.

10 True or false: Mariner 4 was the first probe to take a picture of Mars?

◆ True

In 1965, Mariner 2 became the first probe to fly past the red planet, sending back close-up images of the Martian surface.

Podium!

Bronze: 1–5 correct answers

Silver: 6–8 correct answers

Gold: 9–10 correct answers

Life in Space

There may be zero gravity in space, but let's hope you get more than zero correct answers here on Earth!

1 True or false: Because of the weightless conditions in space, everything drops to the ground.
- ◆ True
- ▲ False

2 Why do astronauts need to exercise in space?
- ◆ To avoid muscle loss
- ▲ To avoid weight gain
- ● To stop them getting bored

3 Can astronauts in space keep in touch with friends and family?
- ◆ No
- ▲ Yes
- ● At certain times of day
- ■ Depends on where they are

4 What does this picture show?
- ◆ Tool kit
- ▲ Tray of food
- ● Toiletries

5 What do astronauts use to wash with?
- ◆ Alcohol
- ▲ Water
- ● Sand

Did you know?

Solid waste from the toilet is compacted and stored in a canister before being either returned to Earth or loaded onto a cargo vehicle bound for burn-up. Urine is recycled into drinking water for use on the spacecraft.

6 In zero gravity, how do astronauts stay on the toilet?
◆ They hold handles.
▲ They use magnets.
● They are strapped in.

7 How long does it take an astronaut to put on a spacesuit?
◆ About 45 minutes
▲ 1 hour
● 2 hours

8 What was The Manned Maneuvring Unit (MMU)?
◆ A small spacecraft
▲ A robot
● A space armchair
■ A long piece of rope

9 How much does a toilet on the ISS cost?
◆ US$9,000 (£7,900)
▲ US$9 million (£7.9 million)
● US$19 million (£16.7 million)

10 True or false: Astronauts sleep floating in the air.
◆ True
▲ False

Scan the QR code for a Kahoot! about life in space.

Turn to page 96 for the answers!

Life in Space
Answers

1 True or false: Because of the weightless conditions in space, everything drops to the ground.
▲ False
Everything floats in space, including astronauts!

2 Why do astronauts need to exercise in space?
◆ To avoid muscle loss
Due to weightlessness, astronauts lose muscle and bone strength so they need to exercise to stay strong.

3 Can astronauts in space keep in touch with friends and family?
▲ Yes
They can use video links, emails, or radio.

4 What does this picture show?
▲ Tray of food
Food is vacuum-packed and cutlery is held in place by magnets. Food can taste more bland in space than on Earth, so spicy dishes are popular.

5 What do astronauts use to wash with?
◆ Alcohol
Water doesn't flow in zero gravity so they wipe themselves with alcohol or a wet towel with liquid soap.

6 In zero gravity, how do astronauts stay on the toilet?

● They are strapped in.

Air flow is used to suck waste into the right place.

7 How long does it take an astronaut to put on a spacesuit?

◆ About 45 minutes

They need at least two people to help them get into the suit.

8 What was The Manned Maneuvring Unit (MMU)?

● A space armchair

Astronauts used these special chairs to fly in space when they needed to do work outside of the spacecraft.

9 How much does a toilet on the ISS cost?

● US$19 million (£16.7 million)

Building a toilet for space is expensive due to the complex waste management system needed, including recycling.

10 True or false: Astronauts sleep floating in the air.

▲ False

They don't sleep floating as they would keep bumping into things! Their sleeping bags, bunk beds, or chairs are attached to something.

Podium!

Bronze: 1–5 correct answers
Silver: 6–8 correct answers
Gold: 9–10 correct answers

Space Shuttles

Shoot for the stars and deliver plenty of correct answers in this quiz!

1 What is the official name for a space shuttle?
- ◆ People Carrier Through Space
- ▲ Celestial Transporter
- ● Space Transportation System

2 When did the first space shuttle launch?
- ◆ 1971
- ▲ 1981
- ● 1991

3 Where were the first space shuttles launched from?
- ◆ India
- ▲ Russia
- ● United States
- ■ China

4 In what order do the three main parts of a shuttle return to Earth?
- ◆ Orbiter
- ▲ External tank
- ● Solid rocket boosters

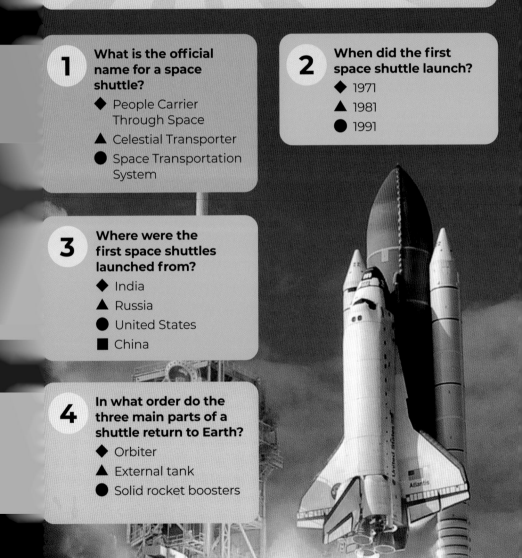

5 True or false: Space shuttles land on Earth like an airplane.
- ◆ True
- ▲ False

6 Which shuttle never flew in space?
- ◆ Enterprise
- ▲ Discovery
- ● Challenger

7 Which shuttle went on its final mission in 2011?
- ◆ Endeavour
- ▲ Atlantis
- ● Challenger

8 What did the shuttle Discovery deliver into space in 1990?
- ◆ James Webb telescope
- ▲ A satellite
- ● Hubble telescope

10 Where did the booster rockets land after takeoff?
- ◆ Atlantic Ocean
- ▲ Grand Canyon
- ● Florida Keys

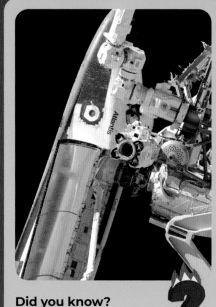

Did you know?

Without space shuttles, the International Space Station (ISS) would not have been built. During 36 missions, the shuttles transported the ISS modules into space, assembled them, delivered supplies, and transported crew.

9 How many flights did the fleet of reusable shuttles make in total?
- ◆ 5
- ▲ 12
- ● 25
- ■ 135

Turn to page 100 for the answers!

Space Shuttles
Answers

1 What is the official name for a space shuttle?
- ● Space Transportation System

A space shuttle is reusable, carrying payloads into space and then returning to Earth.

2 When did the first space shuttle launch?
- ▲ 1981

The first shuttle mission into space was Columbia on April 12, 1981.

3 Where were the first space shuttles launched from?
- ● United States

The launch site was Kennedy Space Center in Florida. A typical mission lasted 12 to 16 days.

4 In what order do the three main parts of a shuttle return to Earth?
- ● Solid rocket boosters
- ▲ External tank
- ◆ Orbiter

The solid rocket boosters separate from the shuttle around two minutes after launch.

5 True or false: Space shuttles land on Earth like an airplane.
- ◆ True

Their wheels come down so they can land on a runway. Brakes and a parachute at the back help to slow them down.

6 Which shuttle never flew in space?

◆ Enterprise

It was only used for testing in the 1970s.

7 Which shuttle went on its final mission in 2011?

▲ Atlantis

Its final payload was an Italian-built cargo module headed for the ISS.

8 What did the shuttle Discovery deliver into space in 1990?

● Hubble telescope

Shuttles allowed the astronauts to repair and maintain the telescope.

9 How many flights did the fleet of reusable shuttles make in total?

■ 135

Six shuttles undertook a total of 135 missions. They were the world's first reusable spacecraft and they operated for 30 years.

Podium!

Bronze: 1–5 correct answers

Silver: 6–8 correct answers

Gold: 9–10 correct answers

10 Where did the booster rockets land after takeoff?

◆ Atlantic Ocean

They were recovered by ships and taken back to the space center to be reused.

History of Space Travel

Will this space travel quiz leave you falling behind?

1 Which country launched the first space station into space?

◆ The US

▲ The UK

● China

■ USSR (what is now Russia)

2 True or false: Astronauts have walked on the Moon and on Mars.

◆ True

▲ False

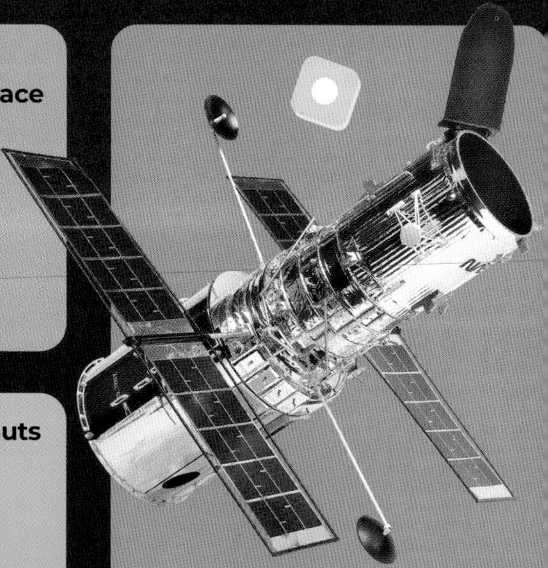

4 Why is the US Apollo 11 mission so famous?

◆ It discovered a new planet nobody knew about.

▲ It made contact with alien life.

● It placed two people on the Moon.

3 What was the name of the telescope sent into space in 1990?

◆ The Bubble Space Telescope

▲ The Rumbling Space Telescope

● The Hubble Space Telescope

■ The Humble Space Telescope

5 True or false: Animals were sent into space before humans.

◆ True

▲ False

6 What was the name of the first artificial satellite to orbit Earth?

◆ Sputnik 1

▲ Sputnik 2

● Sputnik 3

7 Which planet did Viking 1 land on in 1976, from which it sent back color images to Earth?

◆ Neptune

▲ Mars

● Venus

■ Pluto

Did you know?

Launching a space shuttle costs US$450 million (£395 million).

8 Which two countries were involved in the Space Race?

◆ The US and the Soviet Union

▲ France and Germany

● The US and the UK

9 Why is Yuri Gagarin from the USSR (now Russia) famous?

◆ He was a rocket scientist.

▲ He's a space robot.

● He was the first human in space.

Scan the QR code for a Kahoot! about the history of space travel.

10 What made history as the biggest human-made structure in space?

◆ International Space Station (ISS)

▲ Sputnik

● Hubble Space Telescope

■ Statue of Yuri Gagarin

Turn to page 104 for the answers!

History of Space Travel
Answers

1 Which country launched the first space station into space?

■ USSR (what is now Russia)

Salyut 1 was launched by the Soviet Union in 1971 and remained in orbit for 175 days.

2 True or false: Astronauts have walked on the Moon and on Mars.

▲ False

The Moon is the only place astronauts have set foot on besides Earth. The very thin atmosphere on Mars is 95 percent carbon dioxide and a complete mission there and back would take two or three years.

3 What was the name of the telescope sent into space in 1990?

● The Hubble Space Telescope

4 Why is the US Apollo 11 mission so famous?

● It placed two people on the Moon

In July 1969, astronauts Neil Armstrong and Buzz Aldrin landed on the Moon and walked on its surface.

5 True or false: Animals were sent into space before humans.

◆ True

In 1947, the United States sent the first animals (fruit flies) into space. They did this to see how the flies would respond to being in space.

6 What was the name of the first artificial satellite to orbit Earth?

◆ Sputnik 1

Sputnik 1 was launched by the USSR (now Russia) on October 4, 1957.

7 Which planet did Viking 1 land on in 1976, from which it sent back color images to Earth?

▲ Mars

The US space robot carried out soil tests, as well as sending pictures of the surface.

8 Which two countries were involved in the Space Race?

◆ The US and the USSR (now Russia)

Lasting for several years during what was known as the Cold War, the two countries raced to be the first nation to put a person on the Moon.

9 Why is Yuri Gagarin from the USSR (now Russia) famous?

● He was the first human in space.

Yuri Gagarin went into space in April 1961 in a vehicle called Vostok 1.

Podium!

Bronze: 1–5 correct answers
Silver: 6–8 correct answers
Gold: 9–10 correct answers

10 What made history as the biggest human-made structure in space?

◆ International Space Station (ISS)

The ISS was built in 1998, and the first humans arrived onboard in 2000.

Space Tourism

Wish you were here?
Well, one day you could be.
3, 2, 1 . . . let's go!

1 **What year was the first tourist flight into space?**
- ◆ 2000
- ▲ 2009
- ● 2010
- ■ 2021

2 **Who is the founder of Virgin Galactic?**
- ◆ Richard Branson
- ▲ Jeff Bezos
- ● Steve Jobs
- ■ Elon Musk

3 **True or false: In 2021 Richard Branson became the first billionaire to launch himself into space.**
- ◆ True
- ▲ False

4 **How much is a Virgin Galactic space tourism ticket expected to cost?**
- ◆ US$250,000 (£220,000)
- ▲ US$300,000 (£263,000)
- ● US$450,000 (£395,000)

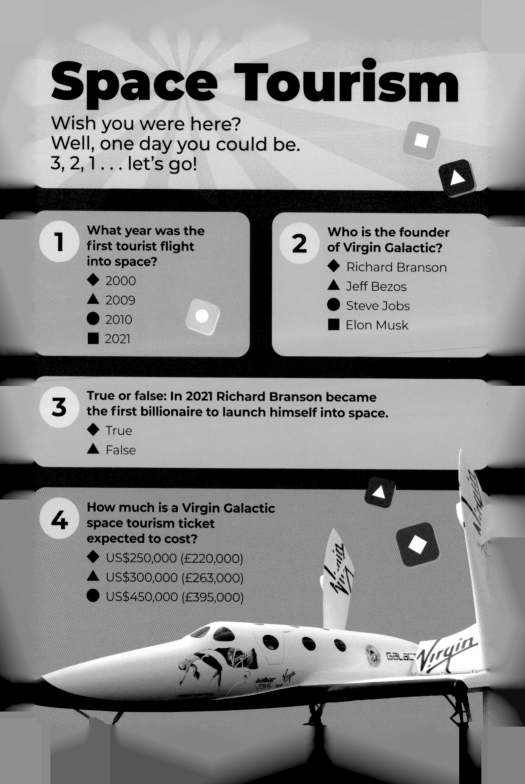

5 Which *Star Trek* actor went into space aboard a rocket in 2021?

◆ Kate Winslet
▲ William Shatner
● Leonard Nimoy

6 True or false: Elon Musk's SpaceX launched a flight with no professional astronauts on board.

◆ True
▲ False

7 Who was the first person to pay for a flight into space?

◆ Dennis Tito
▲ Kayla Barron
● Matthias Maurer

8 How much prize money was offered in 2004 for building a spaceship that would fly above 62 miles (100 km) twice within two weeks?

◆ US$10 million (£8.75 million)
▲ US$100 million (£87.5 million)
● US$10 billion (£8.75 billion)

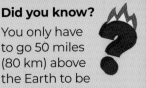

Did you know? You only have to go 50 miles (80 km) above the Earth to be in space!

9 What is the New Shepard?

◆ A rocket for taking sheep to space
▲ A reusable rocket that can take six passengers
● A design for a new space station

10 What was launched into space during Falcon Heavy's test flight in 2018?

◆ A statue of Elon Musk
▲ A bunch of flowers
● An electric car

Turn to page 108 for the answers!

Space Tourism
Answers

1 What year was the first tourist flight into space?

■ 2021

Space tourism is still very new. Virgin Galactic, Blue Origin, and SpaceX all flew their first tourist missions in 2021.

2 Who is the founder of Virgin Galactic?

◆ Richard Branson

The British entrepreneur is founder of the Virgin Group. It is one of the world's most famous brands and includes Virgin Atlantic Airways.

3 True or false: In 2021 Richard Branson became the first billionaire to launch himself into space.

◆ True

His company had been developing the vehicle for 17 years.

4 How much is a Virgin Galactic space tourism ticket expected to cost?

● US$450,000 (£395,000)

The 90-minute flight is promised to include the experience of weightlessness and incredible views.

5 Which *Star Trek* actor went into space aboard a rocket in 2021?

▲ William Shatner

The actor played Captain James T. Kirk on *Star Trek: The Original Series*. At 90 years old, he was also the oldest person to have flown to space.

6 True or false: Elon Musk's SpaceX launched a flight with no professional astronauts on board.

◆ True

In 2021, the Inspiration4 mission took four civilians into space on a three-day mission.

7 Who was the first person to pay for a flight into space?

◆ Dennis Tito

The American millionaire businessman flew on a Soyuz spacecraft to the ISS, arriving on April 30, 2001.

8 How much prize money was offered in 2004 for building a spaceship that would fly above 62 miles (100 km) twice within two weeks?

◆ US$10 million (£8.75 million)

The prize was from the X Prize Foundation and was won by SpaceShipOne, a three-seat spaceplane which has since been scaled up by Virgin Galactic.

9 What is the New Shepard?

▲ A reusable rocket that can take six passengers

It was built by Jeff Bezos's Blue Origin company.

10 What was launched into space during Falcon Heavy's test flight in 2018?

● An electric car

The SpaceX rocket carried a payload of a car with a mannequin in a spacesuit behind the wheel.

Podium!

Bronze: 1–5 correct answers
Silver: 6–8 correct answers
Gold: 9–10 correct answers

Rovers

Having a rocky ride? Never fear . . . a few bumps in the road are all part of the fun in this next quiz.

1 Why are rovers different to other spacecraft?
- ◆ Rovers play music as they move.
- ▲ Rovers can move around once they land.
- ● Rovers carry more people.

2 How many rovers has NASA sent to Mars?
- ◆ One
- ▲ Five
- ● Nine

3 What happens when a rover runs into bumpy ground?
- ◆ It gets stuck.
- ▲ It takes off and flies over them.
- ● It rides over the bumps.

4 In what year was the first rover sent to Mars?
- ◆ 1997
- ▲ 2004
- ● 2012

5 Rovers can be as big as . . .
- ◆ A pet cat
- ▲ A car
- ● An airplane

6 How long does it take a message from a Mars rover to reach Earth?
- ◆ 2 minutes
- ▲ 20 minutes
- ● 1 hour
- ■ 2 hours

7 What is Ingenuity?
- ◆ A rover on skis
- ▲ A crater on Mars
- ● A Mars helicopter

8 True or false: The rover Opportunity landed on Mars in 2004 and is still working there today.
- ◆ True
- ▲ False

Did you know?

Mars rovers are designed with six wheels that each have a separate electric motor. This means that if one wheel gets stuck or a motor breaks down, the rover can still keep moving.

9 How long is the journey from Earth to Mars?
- ◆ 3 months
- ▲ 7.5 months
- ● 10 months

10 Why do rovers have "hazcams" attached to them?
- ◆ To film them crashing into obstacles
- ▲ To take snaps of their favorite moments
- ● To help them avoid any obstacles

Scan the QR code for a Kahoot! about rovers.

Turn to page 112 for the answers!

Rovers
Answers

1 **Why are rovers different to other spacecraft?**

▲ Rovers can move around once they land.

Most spacecraft stay in one spot when they land, but rovers are designed to explore, driving to destinations picked by scientists on Earth.

Opportunity Rover

2 **How many rovers has NASA sent to Mars?**

▲ Five

The names of the five rovers are Sojourner, Spirit, Opportunity, Curiosity, and Perseverance.

3 **What happens when a rover runs into bumpy ground?**

● It rides over the bumps.

The wheels are cleverly designed with a system that adjusts to roll over bumps. The rover stays steady at all times.

4 **In what year was the first rover sent to Mars?**

◆ 1997

Sojourner was the first robot on wheels to rove the cold and dusty planet Mars.

5 Rovers can be as big as . . .

▲ A car

Rovers range from as small as a microwave oven to as big as a car. They're packed with scientific instruments including an internal computer that is the rover's "brain."

Curiosity Rover

6 How long does it take a message from a Mars rover to reach Earth?

▲ 20 minutes

Rovers use radio antennae to send data back to Earth.

7 What is Ingenuity?

● A Mars helicopter

Ingenuity was carried aboard Perseverance and it made more than 30 flights to explore the landscape around the rover.

8 True or false: The rover Opportunity landed on Mars in 2004 and is still working there today.

▲ False

Opportunity finally stopped working in 2018, after traveling across 28 miles (45 km) of Martian terrain.

9 How long is the journey from Earth to Mars?

▲ 7.5 months

The distance between Earth and Mars changes because they orbit the Sun at different speeds.

10 Why do rovers have "hazcams" attached to them?

● To help them avoid any obstacles

"Hazcams" are hazard avoidance cameras that help rovers map the terrain in their path.

Podium!

Bronze: 1–5 correct answers
Silver: 6–8 correct answers
Gold: 9–10 correct answers

Famous Faces of Space

Each of these astronauts has a claim to fame, but do you know what it is?

1 **Who was the second person to walk on the moon?**
- ◆ Buzz Aldrin
- ▲ Neil Armstrong
- ● Jim Lovell

2 **Yuri Gagarin was the first astronaut in space, but where was he from?**
- ◆ USSR (Russia)
- ▲ United States
- ● Australia
- ■ China

3 **True or false: Neil Armstrong's quote when landing on the moon was: "That's one giant step for a man, one small leap for mankind."**
- ◆ True
- ▲ False

4 **What year was the famous first moon landing?**
- ◆ 1959
- ▲ 1969
- ● 1979

Did you know?
The name "astronaut" comes from the Greek words for "star" and "sailor."

5 Why is Valentina Tereshkova famous?

- ◆ She invented the Hubble Telescope.
- ▲ She walked on Mars.
- ● She was the first woman in space.

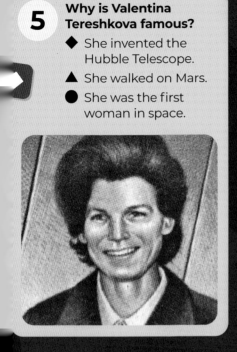

6 Along with Buzz Aldrin and Neil Armstrong, who was the third astronaut on the Apollo 11 mission?

- ◆ Michael Collins
- ▲ Michael Jordan
- ● Jim Lovell
- ■ Valeri Polyakov

7 What unusual action on the moon made Alan Shepard famous?

- ◆ Doing a cartwheel
- ▲ Playing tennis
- ● Hitting a golf ball
- ■ Doing a little dance

8 Put these astronauts in the order they went into space.

- ◆ Valentina Tereshkova
- ▲ Yang Liwei
- ● Neil Armstrong
- ■ Yuri Gagarin

9 What is cosmonaut Valeri Polyakov famous for?

- ◆ Making the quickest journey to the Moon
- ▲ The shortest trip to space
- ● The longest stay in space
- ■ The first person to sneeze in space

10 Why were Belka and Strelka unusual spacecraft passengers?

- ◆ They were scared of flying.
- ▲ They were children.
- ● They were dogs.

Turn to page 116 for the answers!

Famous Faces of Space

Answers

1 Who was the second person to walk on the moon?

◆ Buzz Aldrin

Buzz Aldrin accompanied Neil Armstrong on the Apollo 11 landing.

2 Yuri Gagarin was the first astronaut in space, but where was he from?

◆ USSR (Russia)

In 1961, Yuri Gagarin travelled in the Vostok 1.

3 True or false: Neil Armstrong's quote when landing on the moon was: "That's one giant step for a man, one small leap for mankind."

▲ False

Neil Armstrong's famous quote when landing on the moon was: "That's one small step for a man, one giant leap for mankind."

4 What year was the famous first moon landing?

▲ 1969

The Lunar Module Eagle landed on July 20, 1969.

5 Why is Valentina Tereshkova famous?

● She was the first woman in space

She flew a solo mission on June 16, 1963.

6 Along with Buzz Aldrin and Neil Armstrong, who was the third astronaut on the Apollo 11 mission?

◆ Michael Collins

His name is often forgotten because he stayed inside the command module when Buzz and Neil walked on the moon.

7 What unusual action on the moon made Alan Shepard famous?

● Hitting a golf ball

The American astronaut was the fifth person to walk on the Moon.

8 Put these astronauts in the order they went into space.

■ Yuri Gagarin (1961)

◆ Valentina Tereshkova (1963)

● Neil Armstrong (1969)

▲ Yang Liwei (2003)

At 26 years old, Tereshkova was the youngest when she traveled into space.

9 What is cosmonaut Valeri Polyakov famous for?

● The longest stay in space

Valeri Polyakov holds the record for the longest time spent in space at 438 days. The stay lasted from January 8, 1994 to March 22, 1995 aboard the Mir space station.

10 Why were Belka and Strelka unusual spacecraft passengers?

● They were dogs.

The pooches travelled on the Sputnik 5 mission, launched in 1960 by the Soviet space program. Strelka went on to have six puppies.

Podium!

Bronze: 1–5 correct answers

Silver: 6–8 correct answers

Gold: 9–10 correct answers

Space Scientists

Find out if you know your Galileo from your Hubble . . .

1 How long did it take people to agree that Earth travels around the Sun, after it was first suggested?

◆ 10 centuries

▲ 14 centuries

● 18 centuries

2 Who proved that the Sun is at the center of the Solar System?

◆ Galileo Galilei

▲ Christiaan Huygens

● Isaac Newton

3 In what year did Dutch astronomer Christiaan Huygens discover the first of Saturn's moons?

◆ 1555

▲ 1655

● 1755

4 How were radio waves coming from space discovered?

◆ With a long-distance radio

▲ Using a homemade aerial

● Bouncing off towers

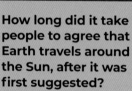

Did you know?

Isaac Newton made the first working reflector telescope in 1668. With it, he could see the four moons of Jupiter.

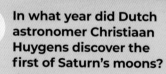

5 Who has a space telescope observatory named after them?
- ◆ Neil Armstrong
- ▲ Edna Dubble
- ● Edwin Hubble

6 Put these events in order:
- ◆ Yuri Gagarin is the first person in space.
- ▲ Edwin Hubble announces the discovery of galaxies beyond our own.
- ● Léon Foucault and Armand Fizeau take the first ever space photographs.

7 What phenomenon does the Bayeux Tapestry show?
- ◆ Halley's comet
- ▲ The first eclipse to be recorded
- ● The first observation of the rings of Saturn

8 Who was known as the "census taker of the sky" in the early 1900s?
- ◆ Annie Jump Cannon
- ▲ Ann Leap-Gunn
- ● Annabel Hop Boom
- ■ Annie Census

9 In what year was Uranus discovered by William Herschel?
- ◆ 1781
- ▲ 1881
- ● 1961
- ■ 1982

10 What was physicist Subrahmanyan Chandrasekhar famous for?
- ◆ Inventing a telescope
- ▲ Going to space
- ● Discovering facts about massive stars

Scan the QR code for a Kahoot! about space scientists.

Turn to page 120 for the answers!

Space Scientists

Answers

1 How long did it take people to agree that Earth travels around the Sun, after it was first suggested?

● 18 centuries

It was suggested by the Greek astronomer Aristarchus of Samos sometime between 320 and 250 BCE.

2 Who proved that the Sun is at the center of the Solar System?

◆ Galileo Galilei

In 1610 he discovered Moon-like phases of Venus, meaning it had to be orbiting the Sun.

3 In what year did Dutch astronomer Christiaan Huygens discover the first of Saturn's moons?

▲ 1655

The European Space Agency's Saturn probe was named after him.

4 How were radio waves coming from space discovered?

▲ Using a homemade aerial

American engineer Karl Jansky discovered them in 1931 while investigating radio interference.

5 Who has a space telescope observatory named after them?

● Edwin Hubble

He proved that there are other galaxies and that they are moving away from each other as the Universe expands.

6 Put these events in order:

- ● Léon Foucault and Armand Fizeau take the first ever space photographs (1845).
- ▲ Edwin Hubble announces the discovery of galaxies beyond our own (1925).
- ◆ Yuri Gagarin is the first person in space (1961).

7 What phenomenon does the Bayeux Tapestry show?

- ◆ Halley's comet

Halley features in the Bayeux Tapestry and appears just before the Battle of Hastings in 1066.

8 Who was known as the "census taker of the sky" in the early 1900s?

- ◆ Annie Jump Cannon

She classified around 350,000 stars manually and developed the Harvard spectral system, which is still used to classify stars today.

9 In what year was Uranus discovered by William Herschel?

- ◆ 1781

Looking through his homemade telescope, he noticed a greenish star that was not shown on his sky charts.

10 What was physicist Subrahmanyan Chandrasekhar famous for?

- ● Discovering facts about massive stars

He showed that when they die, they collapse in supernova explosions to form dense neutron stars or black holes.

Podium!

Bronze: 1–5 correct answers

Silver: 6–8 correct answers

Gold: 9–10 correct answers

Record Breakers

Get busy with these questions because they won't be the records for long!

1 Who was the first person to walk on the moon?
- ◆ Buzz Aldrin
- ▲ Neil Armstrong
- ● Yuri Gagarin

2 What record breaker can you see here?
- ◆ Voyager 2
- ▲ The ISS
- ● Hubble Telescope

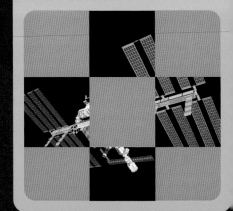

3 What is the brightest star in the night sky?
- ◆ The North Star
- ▲ Sirius
- ● Canopus
- ■ Betelgeuse

4 Which is the fastest spacecraft?
- ◆ Parker Solar Probe
- ▲ Voyager 1
- ● Luna 24
- ■ The space shuttle

5 How tall was Saturn V, the largest rocket ever built?

◆ 166 ft (50.6 m)

▲ 363 ft (110.6 m)

● 494 ft (150.6 m)

6 What was the lunar speed record set in 1972?

◆ 11.2 mph (18 kph)

▲ 17.4 mph (28 kph)

● 23.6 mph (38 kph)

7 True or false: The James Webb Space Telescope is bigger than the Hubble Space Telescope and will become its successor.

◆ True

▲ False

8 What's the longest distance covered by a rover?

◆ 22 miles (35.4 km)

▲ 28 miles (45 km)

● 37 miles (60 km)

9 What is the highest number of applicants for astronaut selection that NASA ever had?

◆ 1,830

▲ 18,300

● 183,000

Did you know?

In 2001, ISS Expedition 2 astronauts James S. Voss and Susan J. Helms conducted a spacewalk for 8 hours and 56 minutes, making it the longest extra-vehicular activity in history.

10 What is the most remote planetary landing so far?

◆ Onto Saturn's moon Titan

▲ Onto Uranus's moon Titania

● Onto Neptune's moon Triton

Turn to page 124 for the answers!

Record Breakers

Answers

1 **Who was the first person to walk on the moon?**
▲ Neil Armstrong
Neil Armstrong's first footsteps on the Moon were taken on July 21, 1969.

2 **What record breaker can you see here?**
▲ The ISS

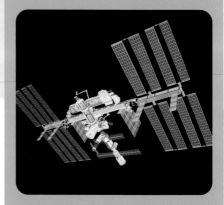

The International Space Station (ISS) is the largest human-made structure in space.

3 **What is the brightest star in the night sky?**
▲ Sirius
Also known as the "Dog Star," Sirius appears bright to us mostly because it's close to Earth.

4 **Which is the fastest spacecraft?**
◆ Parker Solar Probe
The probe reached a speed of 364,620 mph (586,800 kph) on November 20, 2021.

5 **How tall was Saturn V, the largest rocket ever built?**
▲ 363 ft (110.6 m)
It weighed as much as 3,268 tons (2,965 tonnes) when fully fueled.

6
What was the lunar speed record set in 1972?

◆ 11.2 mph (18 kph)

US astronauts Eugene Cernan and Harrison Schmitt reported getting their Lunar Roving Vehicle up to the record-breaking speed.

7
True or false: The James Webb Space Telescope is bigger than the Hubble Space Telescope and will become its successor.

◆ True

Launched in 2021, it is expected to become the dominant observatory for the next 20 years.

8
What's the longest distance covered by a rover?

▲ 28 miles (45 km)

The NASA rover, Opportunity, slowly rumbled along Mars between 2004 and 2018, until a dust storm stopped it.

9
What is the highest number of applicants for astronaut selection that NASA ever had?

▲ 18,300

In 2015, the recruitment process for Astronaut Group 22 started. The applicants were whittled down to just 12 people. The previous record was 8,000 applicants in 1978 for Astronaut Group 8.

10
What is the most remote planetary landing so far?

◆ Onto Saturn's moon Titan

It's 869 million miles (1.4 billion km) from the Sun. In 2005, the unmanned probe Cassini deployed a lander called Huygens.

Podium!

Bronze: 1–5 correct answers
Silver: 6–8 correct answers
Gold: 9–10 correct answers

Glossary

Asteroid

Small rocky object that orbits the Sun, like a planet does.

Comet

Snowball of frozen gas, rock, and dust orbiting the Sun. It heats up and glows when orbiting closer to the Sun.

Crater

A big cavity on a planet's surface in the shape of a bowl. They're usually caused by an explosion or the impact of a meteorite.

Gibbous

When more than half of the Moon's face can be seen. A Gibbous Moon is the phase both just before and after a Full Moon.

Humanoid

A robot with a human shape including legs so that it can do certain tasks with ease.

Mantle

The layer inside a planet found between the core and the crust of rock or ice.

Probe

An artificial satellite that travels in orbit collecting scientific data.

Rover

Exploration vehicles designed to move across the solid surface on a planet.

Satellite

A moon, planet, or machine that orbits a planet or star. Artificial satellites or machines are sent into space for many reasons, such as weather forecasting or to gather data.

Supermassive

A very large mass. It can refer to both black holes and stars.

Supernova

A supernova is a mega explosion that happens when a star suddenly collapses. It can light up the Universe for days.

White dwarf

This is the name given to a star in the final stage of its life cycle when the atoms inside it no longer give it energy.